VALERIY TARSIS   RUSSIA AND THE RUSSIANS

Valeriy Tarsis

Russia and the Russians

Translated by Ilse Barker

Macdonald: London

Contents

356 02926 3
© Copyright 1967
by Verlag C. J. Bucher,
Lucerne and Frankfort/M
This translation ©
Macdonald & Co.
(Publishers) Ltd., 1970
First published
in Great Britain in 1970 by
Macdonald & Co.
(Publishers) Ltd.,
St. Giles House,
49/50 Poland Street,
London, W. 1.
Printed in Switzerland

Prologue

In some Russian fairy tales we meet a friendly, lightfooted little horse whose name is Gorbunok, and in my imagination I am going to saddle it to set off on a long journey, a ride through the space and time of thousand-year-old Russia. The journey will take me along broad highways but also by winding by-roads, along precipitous mountain paths, through the narrow rides of dark forests, a journey beside wild torrents and lazy, broad rivers, and on the banks of dark-blue lakes and inland seas. And I shall be the lonely rider on the Taurian shore, keeping a look-out to seek, in my own fashion, 'with my soul the land of the Greeks' which means the land that all human beings carry within their hearts, the land of freedom and a free mankind.... And riding on, my soul will meet heroes and saints and robbers, and the *rebiata,* the gay companions of Russian folk song who court the robust, full-bosomed girls of Russian villages and Russian poetry.

But Gorbunok will also have to trot through the heat of the steaming steppes of Uzbekistan and rest at dusk beside the camp fires of Caucasian herdsmen and story-tellers. Russia is large, it spans a sixth of the earth, and therefore its diversity is unequalled. Gorbunok will therefore also venture into the tundra, the eternal winter of Kamchatka and Yakutia, where the long polar night descends for many months on a region as large as the whole of Western Europe. Horse and rider will return to the old cities of Novgorod and Suzdal, to Vladimir and Kiev, and to the Holy Moscow of the Boyars. They will hasten through the modern Moscow of the Soviets, changed by the metamorphosis of the Revolution. In today's Leningrad, the city which, for over two hundred years, bore the name of its founder, they will encounter the Russian dream of beauty and splendour, a dream of open communication with the rest of the world, a dream of freedom....

The reality of Russia surpasses every flight of the imagination. The wealth of the Russian earth alone is immeasurable, in the true sense of the word. The gigantic mountain ranges of the Urals hold a multitude of ores and metals, whole treasure-chambers of precious stones such as can be found nowhere else in the world in such profusion. Wherever one digs in the infinite spaces of Russia, from the Danube to the Urals, on the steppes, over the boundless spaces of Siberia, on the chains of hills and in the jungles of the Far East, everywhere there are rich deposits of ores, coal, oil, gold, copper and rare metals, whole subterranean seas of hot water and thousands of mineral springs. Everywhere there are endless forests of deciduous trees and forests of conifers, as well as virgin forests which no man has ever trodden. Every year geological expeditions discover new veins of ore, oil and coal, new deposits of gold, and 5 medicinal springs. In spite of Soviet technology it seems impossible to exhaust the natural wealth of the country, there being neither hands nor heads enough to master it.

The nature of the Russian and his history are as rich as the Russian earth. A characteristic of this history is the danger which continually threatened Russian life, from without and from within. Intruders from the east and the west have harassed and devastated my home land. The Russian steppes and fields, villages and cities have been overrun by the hordes of Attila, Genghis Khan and Batu Khan. Later there was much bloodshed when many parts of the Russian territories were laid waste by the armies of Napoleon, Kaiser Wilhelm II and Hitler. The Russian people have paid for their survival with unimaginable sorrows.

The other, no less threatening danger to 'Russia's inimitable face' arises out of Russia herself. To understand this, one has to judge the events since 1917 from the depth of Russian history to understand that, through the Revolution, Russia's holiest concept, *Freedom,* was endangered. The rebellious, obstinate soul of our people has always passionately longed for it. This yearning was used and misused as a driving force by the organizers of the Revolution who knew well enough their own purpose. And soon afterwards the Communists, through Stalin, established a tyrannical system which obliterated every free impulse of life. Millions of Russia's best sons vanished into prisons and concentration camps.

Noble Russian Horsemen in Tartar habit. (After a contemporary wood-cutting.)

At the beginning of the 19th century, the great poet Alexander Pushkin said: 'Here there is the Russian spirit, here I can smell Russia....' to characterize the freedom-loving attitude of the simple Russian people. In this century they have driven this national spirit out of my homeland. It doesn't smell of Russia any more, rather of Smerdyakov, Dostoevsky's caricature of the Russian. But Russia wasn't famous for its Smerdyakovs after all. And its spirit is not godless but Christian, Orthodox. The great Russian books have made accessible the unsuspected expanses of the Russian personality, their lofty flights and headlong falls, their emotional contradictions, their road in the search for Truth and Right, the gigantic scale of their passions. It is not an accident that it was in Russia rather than in some other country that the race of the 'Seekers after Truth' originated. They roamed through Holy Russia with pilgrim's staffs, supporting themselves by accepting charitable gifts and occasional work, sleeping in hayricks or in the forests by a big camp fire when they were in groups, or by a very small fire when they were alone. They made a simple soup in their kettle, dried their foot bandages and their washing at the fire. They covered thousands of *wersts* on foot, reached far-away monasteries by seldom used roads, to make their obeisance before the miraculous icon of the Mother of God of Potchayev, our succour in all trouble. They went to the Lake of Svetlo where they believed they could hear, rising from its depths at night, the ringing of the bells of the legendary town of Kitesh. And it seemed to them that the virgin Fevronya walked beside them on the green shimmering meadows. If wood goblins mocked these godfearing souls, the pilgrims chased them away by vehemently making the sign of the cross. And in the silent woods, towering castles and palaces appeared to them in which beautiful princesses lived. The miraculous Vassilissa appeared to them, irradiated by the light of the moon and glittering with ice-cold morning dew.

Our race of truth-seekers arises again today. It advances towards a better future in the belief in God and the bright road forward for Russia. I look upon my country with new hope; it will be resurrected and will rise, like a phoenix out of the ashes, spreading its wings for new and lofty flights.

Every unprejudiced person will believe in Russia's future, if he considers her past with attentive consideration, comparing that which once was with that which is. He must look not only into the Russian State but into the Russian soul and into the mirror of that soul, Russian art, literature and philosophy. Then he will immediately be convinced that from the very beginnings of its existence, constantly, passionately, full of contradictions but without ceasing, Russia has been seeking the way to God, the true, deep faith. The Russian people have never been content with any golden mean. They have never made their ideal the complacency of the successful bourgeois, for whom only comfort and satiety is important, and whose Sunday visit to church represents a social decorum empty of religious truth.

Not surprisingly there is nowhere in the world that has produced as many sects as Russia, from the hermits who have retired from the world, the Skoptsky who have voluntarily renounced the most precious gifts of nature, to the Dukhobors or the flagellants who venerate their 'Mother of God' ecstatically, and to whom from time to time she appears to the senses as a radiant young beauty.

Atheism of the western kind has always been deeply alien to the Russian people and remains alien today, although the present Soviet rulers founded the contemporary State and current social order on a Marxist-atheist basis. Russian atheism, and therefore also Soviet atheism, always had, and has still, a philosophical character. Dostoevsky has shown us this typically Russian 'atheist' in the figure of Ivan Karamazov and he turns out to be the passionately religious person apparent in Ivan's narrative *The Grand Inquisitor,* a person indignant that the Christian Church has so imperfectly brought about a realization of its message of divine freedom for mankind in this world. Ivanesque atheism is an existential protest charged with emotion and therefore not an abstract philosophy, but a fundamentally religious attitude. All great Russian thinkers have been religious. Throughout all representative works of Russian poets and philosophers there breathes the spirit of devout Russia. The battle between faith and atheism, between rationalism and mystic truth which, but little noticed by the external world, is being fought in Russia, represents an especially important phase of the development and self-realization of the Russian people. Just as one cannot rationally fully understand the Russia of the icon painters, so other historical and present-day episodes of Russian life are not easily comprehensible to western intellectual thought.

Russia's Secret

The face of Russia, my country, is shadowed with secrets, and one of its strangest riddles is the rôle which orthodoxy has played in the development of the Russian State and the life of its people.

The Russian State had its beginnings in the city of Novgorod, north of Lake Ilmen. From early times Novgorod belonged to the community of cities which stretched from the Baltic to the Black Sea. These cities, probably more than three hundred, were independent communities organized largely on democratic principles and communal economy. There was no organized overall cohesion. Through this territory ran the great universal trade route from Novgorod to the Black Sea, which led 'from the Varangian to the Greeks' and linked northern Europe with Byzantium. The northern centre of trade was 'Great Novgorod'.

The ancient *Chronicle of Nestor* recounts in legendary form that at the beginning of the 9th century the inhabitants of Novgorod decided that their country was large and wealthy, but that 'order' was lacking, and to remedy this they called in the Varangians, known as 'strict people', and bade them take care of public order in Novgorod.

The Varangians, known in European history as the Norman founders of many states, came to power in Novgorod in 862. Thus the Varangian Prince Ryurik founded a dynasty which determined Russia's fate until 1598 when it became extinct, and was followed by the Romanov Dynasty. From Novgorod the whole region of the community of cities was conquered, and in the time of Ryurik's son, the 'hero' Igor, Kiev became the political centre of the Varangian state. Igor and his wife Helga, who changed her name to the Russian Olga, tried to incorporate Byzantium in their empire. Since then it has been the dream of all the Princes of Kiev, and later of the Tsars, until the days of the October Revolution, to conquer 'Tsargrad' (Constantinople), and thus become the acknowledged heirs of 'Eastern Rome'. It remained a dream, but the state of Kiev approached Byzantium ever closer. Impressed by the Byzantine example, a stable government was established, and, at the same time, the cultural and artistic traditions of Byzantium were taken over, a factor which determined the face and the fate of Russia for all time.

Detail of an icon: St. Helena, mother of the Roman Emperor Constantine, founder of the city of Constantinople. Both in religious and political matters, Russia has always felt herself to be the heir of Eastern Rome. The subjects and form of her religious art were inspired by Byzantine models.

▷

The chronicles, so ornamented with legends, which tell us of the introduction of Christianity into the state of Kiev, are psychologically most revealing. It is said that in 985 representatives of the Mohammedan, Roman Catholic, Jewish and Greek-Orthodox faith appeared before Vladimir, each one at pains to win the Russian Prince to his creed. The Byzantine missionary, a skilled dialectitian, came off best in this

competition. Upon his departure Vladimir presented him with gifts and honours, without becoming a Christian himself, however. But two years later, at the suggestion of the Boyars and town elders of Kiev, he decided to send ten reliable and clear-sighted men to investigate the various forms of worship. On their return the envoys gave a detailed account. Charmed by the beauty of Byzantine worship, which had been celebrated with great pomp in their honour at Constantinople, they pleaded the cause of the Greek creed. In 989 a mass christening of the Russian population took place in the waters of the Dniepr. After the destruction of all idols and heathen places of worship, Christian churches were built in Kiev, under the instruction of Greek architects, in those places where the idols had been. Priests from Greece and Bulgaria arranged public worship. Schools were opened to train local priests, and Vladimir arranged for children of aristocratic families (by force, when necessary) to be trained there. The spread of Christianity throughout the whole Kiev state proceeded peacefully. Only at Novgorod, whose inhabitants tried to adhere to their traditional beliefs, was force used. Soon after his death on 15th July 1015, Prince Vladimir was canonized by the Greek Church and became part of Russian popular belief as 'Saint Vladimir'.

His son, Yaroslav the Wise, continued his father's work. Many more churches were built, among them the Cathedral of St. Sophia which still stands today. With its thirteen domes it is, though an adaptation of the Hagia Sophia in Constantinople, the greatest single masterpiece of ancient Russian architecture. The famous Kiev monastery of the caves was also begun at this time. It developed into its impressive and complicated structure from a single monk's cell.

It is characteristic of those times that Yaroslav's grandson, Vladimir Monomakh (he reigned from 1113 to 1125) appears in the chronicles as the perfect example of a peace-loving Christian Prince, although he made war not only on the Infidels, but also on the West-Slavonic nations. Such deviations from the ideal are put down by a contemporary chronicler to the 'intrigues of the adversary'.... The status of 'orthodox ruler' symbolized the subjugation of the world under the cross, and the Church regarded secular Princes as 'architects of the Kingdom of God on earth'. But the sense of a 'stable harmony' between Church and State was lost soon after this.

After the 12th century the glory of the Kiev state began to fade. Disputes about succession, feuds among the principalities, but chiefly the invasion by the Tartars, broke the power of Kiev as a capital. Around 1240 the hordes of Batu Khan conquered Kiev and sacked it. The native Princes soon came back to power, but it had to be ratified by the Khan. Thus Alexander Nevski established himself in 1242, after his victories over his non-orthodox western neighbours, the Swedes and later the Teutonic Knights, as Prince by the Grace of the Khan in the city of Vladimir. Th change in character of the state, by the moving of the capital from Kiev to Vladi and soon after to Moscow, was at the same time given a spiritual significance b appointment of a Metropolitan at Vladimir and his translation to Moscow in Under Ivan Kalita, who became Prince of Vladimir and Moscow in 1322, the t of the new state grew considerably. The occupying Tartars were intereste the payment of tribute, they did not hinder the development of the state a in any way concern themselves with the Church. Thus the Church's au the spiritual and secular wealth of the monasteries) was able to develop u

In 862 the Norman Varangian Prince Ryurik came to power in Novgorod and founded the dynasty which later produced the Tsars. The last representative of the Ryurik dynasty on the throne of the Tsars was Ivan IV, called 'the Terrible'. With his feeble-minded son Fyodor, the house of Ryurik died out.

Tsar Ivan III, called 'The Great', reigned from 1462 to 1505. He was the first to call himself 'Tsar of all Russia'. Under his crown he incorporated all the Russian Princely States in one centrally governed, single state.

This was especially important when the Church's position as the only representative of Orthodoxy was threatened by the *rapprochement* of the Eastern and Western Church in the Union of Florence.

Ivan III, who considered himself the spiritual heir of the Byzantine Empire, and who was the first to rule autocratically as *'Tsar by the Grace of God'* (from 1462 to 1505), not only trebled the territory of Muscovite Russia by wars and clever diplomatic moves; it was also during his reign that the power of the three Khans was broken and the remainder of the Golden Horde destroyed. And above all, by marrying the last successor to the Byzantine throne, Sophia Paleolog, he sealed the claim making Moscow the *Third Rome*. Accordingly the capital was enlarged and embellished, the foundations of the three hundred and fifty churches were laid, and the court developed Byzantine pomp....

At this time there were people in Moscow and Ryazan, in Rostov and Vladimir, who set out secretly and quietly in their straw shoes, moving along snowy and icy paths into the woods of Murom, into the southern Russian and Bashkir steppes. They did not care for the glory of the secular and spiritual Princes. In this way the future Cossacks were born. Thus the sects of the flagellants, the Skoptsky, the sabbath fasters, the Dukhobors were created, and the endless road of the Russian God-seekers began....

It can be seen how hopeless the conception of a 'Third Rome' and 'Holy Russia' made the position of the Church, controlled by the 'most Christian of all rulers'. True, the despotic tyrant Ivan the Terrible (1533 to 1584) made good political use of his sonorous titles: after an unsuccessful attempt to penetrate as far as the Baltic, he 'liberated' the 'true believers' in the south-west from Lithuanian Catholicism, and in the south-east from the yoke of the Moslems. But he wasn't really thinking of the exercise of justice! Towards the end of the 15th century, Ivan III was rebuked by his Archbishop. At the beginning of the 16th century, Vasili still allowed unsolicited advice to come from an abbot. After that, critics of the autocrat had to find more devious outlets. At the time of Ivan the Terrible, the Metropolitan Philipp complained: 'In all countries, even the heathen lands, there is justice and law. Only in Russia there is none.'

The end of the Ryurik dynasty and the ensuing 'time of troubles' until the installation of the Romanovs (1613) encouraged the eruption of smouldering discontent in all sections of society. The 17th century brought the serfdom of the peasants and [viole]nt Cossack risings (under Khmelnitsky in White Russia, under Stenka Rasin in [the Volga]-Don area). True, Boris Godunov's success (1596 to 1605) in establishing [the famo]us Moscow Patriarchate had a stabilizing influence. But in 1666 the [reform o]f the Patriarch Nikon produced a schism which remains to this day. ['Third Rome', was rent in two. The rift between the official Ortho-] [dox and Old] Believers created innumerable new dissidents. In the name [he merc]ilessly persecuted the Old Believers, since they personi-

[17 0]2 to 1725) the Tsar's power encroached decisively [on the Orth]odox Church. Since Peter recognized the Church as an [obstacle i]n his westerly oriented innovations with disfavour, he [abolished an]d put in his place a College of Bishops, the 'Holy Synod',

RUSSIA'S BIRTHPLACE

Page 11:
The city of Novgorod
on the River Volkhov is one
of Russia's oldest cities.
Through Ryurik and his
heirs, the Russian Tsardom
was founded.
In the Middle Ages the
city flourished economically.
The Cathedral of
St. Sophia, built between
1045 and 1050, bears
witness to this. The
remaining ancient buildings
were destroyed in the
Second World War.

Pages 12/13:
Kiev bears the proud name
of 'Mother of Russian
Cities'. Already in the
9th century, Kiev began to
subjugate the surrounding
countryside and to build up
its power. The successors of
Ryurik moved their capital
from Novgorod to Kiev.
After Christianization
an epoch of grandiose
building began.
The Cathedral of St. Sophia,
built in 1037, was a
symbol of the consummation
of the union of Church and
State. Today this city of
millions, which was much
damaged during the War,
is the political, economic
and the cultural centre
of the Republic of the
Ukraine.

supervised by a secular power. The Church had to be subservient to his bureaucratic police state. Like other Tsars after him, Peter, despite his anti-clericalism, fought under the banner of the defence of Orthodoxy, and, invoking this mission, he won access to the Baltic. He put a seal on this enterprise with the foundation of his new capital on the Neva.

Further 'pious' expansions of territory took place under Catherine II (1762 to 1796). In the partition of Poland, Prussia, Austria, White Russia and the Tsarist Empire acquired territories. The Turks had to give up Asov and the coast of the Black Sea, the neutral Crimea fell later 'automatically' to Russia. In the Crimean war (1853 to 1856) under Nicholas I and Alexander II, Russia's position received a setback since the Black Sea became neutral territory, and the Christian subjects of the Sultan came under the protection not only of Russia, but of France and England also. Alexander II carried the Russian people's 'civilizing mission' to Central Asia, and in this way the huge territory of Turkestan became part of the Russian State. He also took an interest in the Slavs under Turkish rule. 'For the sake of the Faith and our Orthodox Brothers', and to raise the cross once again on Hagia Sophia in Constantinople, he sent, in 1877, an army of 'liberation' against the Sultan. The Balkan states were also helped towards independence, but with the Berlin Congress, the Western Powers checked Russia's messianic designs: the European balance of power was at stake.

After the success of the French Revolution, there was ferment and turmoil around the throne of the Tsars. The intelligentsia demanded the emancipation of the peasants and, at the very least, the transformation of the Tsar's power into a constitutional rule. In 1848 Nicholas went to the aid of the Hapsburg monarchs against the Hungarian revolt, while at home his supporters tried to stem the revolutionary flood with the magic formula: 'Orthodoxy, Autocracy and Nationalism.' They tried to stem it chiefly by autocratic measures. Nicholas' successors however, felt themselves forced, if not to limit their autocracy, at least to allow some reforms. The Orthodox Church at any rate gave unconditional support to the autocrats, blessing whatever they undertook. What else could they do? The Chief Procurator of the Holy Synod (a Procurator appointed by the State) Pobedonostsev (1827 to 1907), for example, started out with the hypothesis that Orthodoxy should serve Russia. He believed that the intelligentsia were dangerous, and that the rural population should be protected from too much education, that the Russian State should be founded on the simple faith of the people who looked up to the Tsar as they did to their God. Ironically, this belief in the *narodinky* (simple people), the name later given to the socialist revolutionaries, does not entirely contradict later sympathies with 'socialist views, deeply rooted in the people'.

Tsar and Church were inextricably chained together. Their historical fate was indivisible. The destroyers of the Tsarist State had therefore to be the destroyers of the Church. Communism in Russia appeared in atheistic guise since the Church, by its allegiance to the power of the Tsar, had betrayed man—and therefore God.

Between Europe and Asia

Russia is part of Europe *and* of Asia. Even at the very outset, her christianization towards the end of the 10th century connected her fate with that of Europe. She took on a Christian rhythm of life. Her mental attitudes and social consciousness evolved along Christian lines. But this statement has to be qualified: Russia will always remain 'Eastern Europe'. Greek Orthodoxy and Byzantine custom determined the beginnings of development towards a specifically Russian life, and for a long time embodied the only foundation of Russian culture.

In the 13th century Russia was threatened from the West for the first time. Fortunately Alexander Nevski (who was later canonized) was an excellent commander-in-chief and strategist. His victory over the Swedes by the Neva made him a hero and established Kiev Russia as a European reality. Thanks to his sophisticated, versatile tactics, Alexander Nevski conquered, two years later, an immensely superior force of invading Teutonic Knights, who were known as Europe's best warriors. His soldiers fought under the watchword: 'God is not in strength but in justice.'

This commander-in-chief excelled also as statesman and diplomat. When, after a long siege, the Tartar hordes of Asia conquered Kiev on 6th December 1240 and soon after established the State of the 'Golden Horde' on the lower Volga, Alexander Nevski accepted the political reality, recognizing the military superiority of the Tartars. As Prince of Vladimir he acknowledged them as overlords, and paid the tribute they demanded. Yet he was able, at this time of Russia's involuntary encounter with Asia, to pursue Russian politics, for the Khan was not interested in such matters. All he wanted was that the secular and clerical dignitaries should acknowledge his claim to authority. And the population suffered his occasional raids with the same equanimity with which they had patiently borne the feuds of native princes.

Not until a century and a half later did Dimitry Donskoy take up arms against the Tartar yoke. With the energetic help of Sergey of Radonesh, the founder of the monastery of the Holy Trinity at Sagorsk not far from Moscow, he defeated the Tartars in 1380 on the banks of the Don. Two years later the counter-blow came. Of all Moscow, only the Kremlin survived it. In 1408 another wave of Mongols overran the Muscovite State and burned down the capital. Despite the strong fortifications customary to a monastery, the Sagorsk monastery fell. It was finally the battle of power amongst the three Khans, of Astrakhan, Kazan and Crimea, in which the Khan of Astrakhan was the vanquished and the Tartars of the Crimea the victors, which made it possible for Russia under Ivan III to become independent in 1502.

Page 17:
Icon of St. Boris and St. Gleb from the School of Novgorod of the mid-15th century. Boris and Gleb, the sons of St. Vladimir, were murdered at the order of their brother Svyatopolk. They suffered their fate without resistance and were honoured by the people as saintly sufferers.

Pages 18/19:
The historical and present-day centre of Moscow is the Kremlin. In the eyes of the world it is the Cathedrals (called Sobors in Russian) which chiefly make the Kremlin one of the most remarkable architectural sites.

Pages 20/21:
Sergeyevo, city of St. Sergius, is the historical name of the town of Sagorsk, forty miles north of Moscow. It bears its present name in memory of the Communist Party secretary V. M. Sagorsk who was assassinated in 1919. Sagorsk is the centre of contemporary church activities in the Soviet Union. The city is the site of the only Russian seminar for priests. This is situated in the Theological Academy built by the Empress Elizabeth.

ъ акаѳіста гда нашегѡ їиса хс҃   стагѡ проро

In the middle of the century, Ivan IV, the Terrible, conquered, with the help of western firearms, the weakened State of the Khan of Kazan. Following the path of the Novgorod trade settlements which had reached as far as the Ob, he penetrated the Siberian Tartar State. In 1582 Yermak and his Cossacks conquered the whole of immense Siberia for Ivan. It was natural for Moscow to welcome such an extension of the State in the East, into the inviting distances of Asia. It is comparable to the advance west of the early American settlers. The new territories would have been well worth the Tsar's undivided attention, but Russia was too deeply involved with her West European neighbours who gave her no rest.

The character of Muscovite Russia changed completely because of the Tartars. They destroyed the trade of the old regime and made Russia into an agrarian country. Razing many towns, they stunted the growth of democratic self-government embodied in the *vetche* (town assembly). And what was most important: centuries of Tartar rule taught Russia despotism. The Khan, though so far away, remained a lasting example for the Moscow Princes. The practice of autocracy which eventually emerged was furthered by the theory of the rôle of the Orthodox ruler: that he is the Lord's anointed and the bearer of the charisma of power; that the souls of his subjects are in his care.

Pages 22/23: In Russia's Orthodox churches the nave is divided from the altar by a wall of paintings, the iconostasis. The religious ceremony, one of the mysteries of faith, must be consummated out of sight. These iconostases are usually richly ornamented, and the individual paintings, the icons, are often covered with decorated sheets of silver.

Page 24: The St. Sergius Holy-Trinity Monastery at Sagorsk is one of the most famous clerical buildings of ancient Russia. It is a holy place still venerated throughout Russia, visited by a never-ending stream of pilgrims who come to pray at the grave of St. Sergius. The iconostasis of the monastery church is particularly famous. It used to contain the unique icon of the Holy Trinity, painted by Andrey Rublev. This icon is now in the Tretyakov Gallery in Moscow.

Peter the Great made every possible use of his autocratic power to open up a reluctant country to Western culture. With his own hands he shaved off the beards of his Boyars, and decreed that they must wear European dress. He placed their sons in the academies he had founded where they learned geometry and navigation. To settle European culture in Russia, Peter brought back scientists and technicians from Western Europe, mainly from Germany. He had learned ship-building in Holland and created the first Russian navy. He reorganized the army completely and gave it the latest weapons. The victory over Sweden at Poltava (1709) gave Russia the military footing of a great European power. This European presence also showed in the inner life of the country. Peter orientated it towards the West. He *Europeanized* Russia.

At the time of Catherine II, Russia (at least its cultured upper class) was chiefly exposed to the influence of French rationalism. The Empress herself corresponded with Voltaire! Beside this, a game of changing alliances was played in the political field, now with Austria, now with Prussia. There were wars against the Turks, against the Poles, and the last remnants of Asiatic expansionist ambition, the Tartars of the Crimea, were destroyed.

Then Europe threatened again. The Emperor Napoleon was certainly not just interested in 'tribute'. Russia felt the spiritual independence of the Tsarist State to be threatened. What had happened at the beginning of the 17th century, happened now. Then, during the anarchic period of the troubles, when Boyars, Cossacks and Poles took part in the battle for the throne, when Moscow was already in the hands of the Catholic King Sigismund, the Russian people followed the call of a simple man, Minin, and Prince Pozharsky, rising under their leadership to drive out the intruder. And thus it was in 1812.

After the French invaders had been beaten and expelled, Russia recollected her own values, and her relationship with Europe became better understood. The Slavophiles wanted to make Russia into a great Orthodox Slavonic State. Their **25** opponents, the 'Westernists' on the other hand, saw Russia's salvation in taking over Western progress. A flood of political, social and utopian thought found enthusiastic adherents amongst the Russian intelligentsia. Restrictive measures against the universities were now added to the merciless administration of the Terror in order to maintain the 'order willed by God', i.e. 'willed by the Tsar'. In the works of Dostoevsky this ideological battle for Russia's future is fixed for ever with the depth and clearsightedness of genius. In his *Diary of a Writer,* Dostoevsky caricatured Russia's relationship with Asia and Europe. For centuries Russia took the greatest trouble to be accepted by her European neighbours as a 'genuine' fellow European. Yet the essence of Russia lies in the very fact that she unites within herself both Europe *and* Asia.

Russia lies *between* Europe and Asia. The first time that Asia turned its great force against the West, Russia, though Europe further west was hostile to her, provided the bulwark against which the Asiatic onslaught exhausted itself. It is significant that Russia was never intellectually involved with Asia. Yet Russia extended her territories across the continent of Asia as far as the Pacific. Siberia is as Russian as White Russia and the Ukraine. Russia confronts Europe from a dominant position, but the East conceals not the Tartar-Mongol but the Chinese power with its population three times that of Russia. And Russia looks towards the West, orientates herself completely in that direction. And still China has not set herself in motion....

Petersburg and Moscow

Moscow in the 16th century. (Contemporary woodcutting.)

Petersburg and Moscow personify an eternal Russian antagonism, the dialectical contradiction in Russia's spiritual and political life.

Petersburg, founded by Peter the Great in 1703, became the gateway through which the West could exert its influence, the entrance gate of enlightenment, of rationalism, of German philosophy, free thought, progress, and the beginnings of the industrial age. Through this gateway the spirit of Voltaire entered Russia and so did that of Lenin, expanding and transforming western Marxism into Leninism to fuse with Russian Messianism, that Messianism which had its home in Moscow.

Moscow was the city of the Boyars, of Orthodoxy, the city of the great Russian spirit, the spacious yet tranquil Russian soul. It was the constant source of the spiritual strength of conservative Russia, the mighty island in the ocean of the Russian State.

While Peter the Great, looking towards Europe from the Schlüsselburg (the Castle of the Key), dreamed of the time when he would not just break through a window, but would use this key to open the door to the West, the eyes and thoughts of the Boyars of Moscow and of Peter's son Alexey turned to the infinite spaces of the East, and saw there the tasks and the future of the Russian Orthodox State.

Moscow had become the capital of a great state and, unlike Kiev, it continued to determine its own fate without rejecting influences from all parts of the country over which it had authority. When the Tsar moved into his newly-built Petersburg palace, Moscow continued as the bureaucratic capital. And ever after, the Tsars were crowned in the Kremlin Church of the old capital: the blessing of holy Moscow could hardly be transferred to Petersburg. Moscow was called the 'city of the forty thousand churches', though a more sober figure would have been four hundred. Today about forty remain.

Yes, Moscow has changed. Once it was known by its 'unchanging face'. Today it has become, especially in its suburbs, the faceless mass of a large city. The two hundred villages of the Podmoskovy (as the surroundings of Moscow were called) have almost totally disappeared. They have been pulled down. Small, ancient wood or brick cottages, falling into disrepair between the high blocks of flats, are the only remaining trace of these villages. It is difficult to believe that this giant city was first mentioned in a record of 1147 as a small fishing village built around a small Kremlin. More than eight centuries have passed and the village has spread itself, like Rome, over seven hills, and now covers about ninety-three square miles. Even in the old town the new Moscow has pushed aside the ancient buildings one by one, and has penetrated the narrow alleys. Without the Kremlin, there would be little in common now between the modern city of millions and the old capital of the nobility and of trade. But the change is not only an outward one: the spirit of the city has been transformed. The old, quiet, easy-going Moscow has vanished. Today it is a busy ant-heap, like any other metropolis.

The history of Moscow and the Kremlin cannot be separated from the history of Russia. How many assaults on the Russian State have the Muscovites had to ward off, or to allow to sweep over them! Amidst the fires of arson and in the tumult of battle the 'Third Rome' was born, the Moscow of the archpriest Avvakum and the great anguished Dostoevsky, the twofold Eurasian soul of Russia. And at a time when many a flourishing town met its downfall, Moscow grew into a capital city. Here the Christian ideal of the brotherhood of nations, and the deep mystical belief in Russia's divine mission, a belief embedded in the national consciousness by the Moscow Prince Dimitry Donskoy and Sergey of Radomesh, played a decisive rôle.

The triangle of the Kremlin beside the Moskva is surrounded by a wall 21 feet thick and over 60 feet high. Nineteen towers guard the Kremlin like sentinels. Everyone knows the Spasskaya Tower with the famous Kremlin clock and the red star at its apex. The Spasskaya Tower and Spassky Gate were named after an icon of the Redeemer *(spassitely)* which was brought from Smolensk in 1638 by the order of Tsar Alexey Mikhailovitch. The Tsar always entered the Kremlin through the Spassky Gate. The Armoury Tower, the Command Tower, Arsenal and Corner Arsenal Tower are names that testify to their military use. But the Tower of the Holy Trinity is the highest of them all. The row of Kremlin towers along the bank of the Moskva is completed by the Blagoveshchenskaya Tower. Blagoveshchenskaya means 'message of salvation'. The tower has withstood the centuries, but the messages of salvation have changed. The Borovitskaya Tower (from *bor,* forest thicket) stands as a witness that here the endless Moscow forests once began. Wolves were known to venture as far as the square.

Red Square, beside the Kremlin wall, is as old as Moscow itself. Originally it was called the Square of the Conflagrations, since the wooden buildings and the market of the White City which adjoined the Kremlin frequently burned down. (Until 1917 eighty per cent of Moscow was built of wood.) Russian history quite literally marched across Red Square. Here, in the place of execution, those fit for military service were called up, here government decrees were made known to the people, here political criminals were executed. In 1671 Stenka Razin was beheaded in Red Square. Here the soldiers of the old Muscovite militia who rebelled against Peter's alien anti-christian creed were massacred. Here the insurgent Cossack from the Urals, Emelyan Pugachov, was led across the square in a cage, and it was here that, in 1917, the young White Russians fought for Russia's future.... Their ashes were scattered to the winds, while the urns of those Bolsheviks not prematurely fallen into disfavour, have been fitted into the wall of the Kremlin, while Lenin can be seen, embalmed 'for all eternity' in his glorious grey and rose-coloured mausoleum.

Cathedrals and palaces rise up within the triangle of the Kremlin. The Soviet Government, entrenched behind the fortress walls, has laid claim chiefly to the most 'useful' of the splendid buildings. In the palace of the Kremlin some ballrooms still stand empty, halls which served the Tsarinas for large receptions. Nobody holds meetings there, they are relics of days dead and gone. This is especially true of the

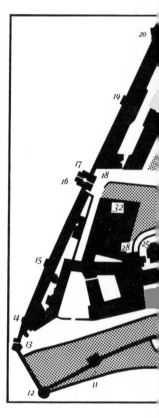

Plan of the Moscow Kremlin

1 Nikolskaya Tower
2 Senate Tower
3 Spasskaya Tower
4 Clock Tower
5 Konstantino-Yeleninskaya Tower
6 Beklemiskevskaya Tower
7 Petrovskaya Tower
8 Second Tower
9 First Tower
10 Secret Tower
11 Annunciation Tower
12 Water Tower
13 Borovitskaya Tower
14 Arsenal Tower
15 Commando Tower
16 Kutafya Tower
17 Bridge of the Holy Trinity
18 Tower of the Holy Trinity
19 Middle Arsenal Tower

chapel where the Tsarina prayed, and of the Golden Chamber where honoured guests were once received.

The whole district adjoining the Kremlin, especially the Saradye, is permeated by the spirit of Muscovite Russia. Here one can still see the arcades of the old market and the churches, built at the beginning of the 19th century in the courtyard of the Andronyevsky monastery. On the banks of the Moskva, opposite the Sperling mountains, rises the Novodevichy Convent, repository of the past and mirror of the present. It has stood there for over four centuries and has shared Moscow's history. Boris Godunov lived there before he was elected Tsar, and so did Peter's first wife as well as his sister who was a pretender to the throne. In the big cemetery lie A. K. Tolstoy, Fadeyev, Mayakovsky, and Stalin's second wife Alliluyeva. Today the Novodevichy Convent, like many other Moscow convents and monasteries, is used for Party purposes.

If one strolls about the city in search of the old Moscow, one will sooner or later come to the Sadovoye Ring (from *sad,* garden). The wall which originally stood here was erected in the 15th century after the Kremlin wall, the Chinese wall and the wall of the White City, to serve as a fourth ring of defence. When Moscow grew in times of peace, the earth wall and the fortifications were cleared away, and the houses of the merchants and residences of the aristocracy were built in their place. The boulevard received its name from their gardens. Towards the end of the Twenties this magnificent ten-mile long avenue was sacrificed to strategic necessities: the boulevard had to be widened to make it practicable for heavy tanks. Recently efforts have been made to embellish the Sadovoye Ring with some greenery once again.

Farther away, in the country surrounding Moscow, lies, to the south, Yasnaya Polyana, country seat of Leo Tolstoy, the great unremitting seeker after truth who inflamed the whole of Russia, and whose invisible presence is still felt today. To the north of Moscow lies Sagorsk and its monastery of the Holy Trinity, probably the most important monastery to survive the October Revolution. About a hundred monks live there today, and in addition a religious academy and a seminary of about three hundred students are attached to the monastery. It was founded in the 14th century and soon became a pillar of the young Muscovite State whose fate it shared. Like a phoenix it has risen from the ashes again and again.

For enemies have ravaged and destroyed Russia from all sides. The country never had friends to depend on, its temporary allies were always themselves a danger. Peter the Great recognized this and decided that Russia must be stronger than her enemies. Then they would of themselves change into friends. At that time Sweden, under Charles XII, was the most powerful state in Europe, and barred Russia's road to the West. But Peter, 'Tsar of all the Russians', saw in his mind's eye a new Amsterdam on the banks of the Neva, a city he would build in the marshes. On Hare Island he laid the foundations of the Peter and Paul fortress and later fortified Kronstadt to enable him to defend Petersburg and the Neva estuary.

From the very beginning Peter shut his eyes to the small wooden town on Vassilyev, Aptekarsky and Yelagin Island. He saw instead a great 'Venice of the North', the most beautiful city in the world with splendid palaces, prospects straight as an arrow, an extensive net of canals spanned by more than six hundred bridges, a city full of lovely churches and a grandiose Senate building.

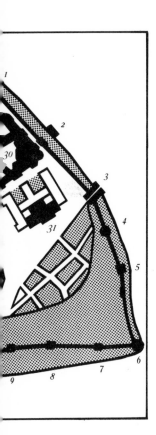

29

The Tsar ordered all the masons in Russia to come to this gigantic building site, and each year as many as forty thousand serfs were brought from all parts of the country to hasten the construction of the city. After the victory of Poltava and the capture of Vyburg (Peter called it 'the solid padding of Petersburg'), and finally after the destruction of the Swedish navy, Petersburg was secure on all sides. Now Peter was able once again to devote all his attention to the building of his new capital. It grew to be the marvel of the whole world. The court of Petersburg became the most splendid in Europe. Never did Moscow know such elegance. But Peter did not crave such magnificence for himself—he wanted all Russia to shine. He sacrificed to Russia all that he had: his genius, his son, his life. On the eve of the execution of his son Alexey, who represented the Moscow claims and who had conspired with the Moscovite Boyars against Peter and his city, the Tsar called to God: 'Lord I believe, help thou my unbelief.' He died in 1725 as a result of an illness he had caught while attempting to save a life in the waters of the Neva in winter.

After Peter, only Catherine II succeeded in increasing Russia's glory during her reign. But she was full of contradictions: an enlightened ruler yet an unbridled woman, a harsh despot but a friend of the Encyclopedists. She built many palaces for her favourites, in and around Petersburg, the greatest of them the Taurida Palace, begun in 1783, built for Prince Potemkin, victor of Tauris (the Crimea). This represents a turning point in architecture, from the pomp of the baroque to the severe simplicity of classicism. Later the Taurida Palace, with its characteristic portals, columns, and triangular pediments became a model not only for the builders of many cities, but also for the architects of the country seats of the nobility, scattered throughout Russia. After the death of Catherine, Paul II, as a revenge on his mother and Prince Potemkin, submitted the palace to a barbaric transformation. He converted it into cavalry barracks. The winter garden was used for stables. Repeatedly reconstructed, the building has, since 1905, housed the then newly-formed Duma*, and has been the witness of a lot of high and noble talk and Bolshevist argument.

The Communists made Moscow the capital again, not, of course, because the spirit of the 'Third Rome', of the city of churches, suited them, but because Leningrad** seemed too exposed, lay too close to the West.... Peter had consciously built it in a provocative, defiant position. And it remains for ever, in the words of Gogol, 'the wonderful chronicle of stone'. St. Petersburg, citadel of Russian greatness, of her will to freedom, will one day carry off the victory over Moscow, of whose character too little remains. There is irony in the fact that the Communists have erected a monument in Leningrad in commemoration of the centenary of the December rising, a revolt against a lack of freedom. The true spirit of Leningrad is preserved in the passion of Gogol and Dostoevsky, and will lead the city and all Russia through tragedy to a purified life.

In the course of his Europeanization, Tsar Peter the Great decreed that his subjects should shave off their beards. Those who wished to keep their beards had to pay a high beard tax. Only clergymen and peasants were allowed to wear beards without paying a tax for them. (Contemporary woodcutting.)

* Russian version of Parliament.

** At the outbreak of the First World War, St. Petersburg was given the Russian name of Petrograd, and in 1924 rechristened Leningrad.

Impressions of Moscow

The wife of Peter III, who had been the German Princess Sophie of Anhalt-Zerbst, sat on the throne of the Tsar after the deposition and death of her husband. She was Catherine II, the Great, and reigned from 1762 to 1796. She was filled with the ideas of French enlightenment. As Tsarina she added to the size and power of the Russian State by victorious wars. (After a painting by Rotari, engraved by Gutenberg.)

Every metropolis sets the tone of the cultural life of its country, and this Moscow has always done for Russia. All intellectual achievement has found immediate response here, whether it is brought to the capital from a National Republic or some small town in the Provinces. Moscow draws to itself whatever is significant in the intellectual and artistic life of Russia. Moscow publishers translate the best books into Russian. The best performances from provincial theatres are shown on the Moscow stage. The best singers, ballerinas and dancers, choirs, ensembles and symphony orchestras from out-lying territories come to Moscow to perform. Most of Russia's important scholars work in Moscow. More than a hundred and twenty thousand students live and study there. Congresses are held, and the central organizations of all the country's cultural organizations are in Moscow. Thirty theatres, more than two hundred cinemas, and about a hundred clubs cater for the entertainment of the Muscovites.

Life here is lived with heightened intensity. The 'genuine' Muscovites, and those who have come to live in the city, have through the centuries given Russia's capital its special character. One encounters their life and work when one takes a walk, no, many walks, through the changed city. Memories arise, joy, sadness, sorrow, hope.

Come with me for such a walk. Let us start at the Kremlin.

The heart of every Russian beats more proudly when he thinks of this incomparable monument to national greatness, and visiting it he experiences a strangely solemn feeling of festivity and awe. At least that is how it was in far-off pre-revolutionary days. Early in the morning one would meet grandmothers and nannies with children there. They walked about as if they were at home, unconstrained and free. After the Revolution, free access was constrained for several decades. The new generation did not see inside it, they looked on it as the castle of some wicked magician holding judgement over their fathers and elder brothers. I remember this terrible time very well. At the beginning of the Thirties, the Tshekists, those evil spirits, nightly took innocent people from their homes and brought them to their dark dungeons. Not one of these unfortunates has ever returned. It was the custom on the next day to declare those who had been arrested 'enemies of the people'. One would no longer greet their wives and children. That was too dangerous. Even a completely casual connection with such an 'enemy of the people' could bring the same fate: to vanish for ever in a concentration camp, or to be shot in the cellars of Varsonovyevsky Street without trial or after tormenting interrogation. And there was no news or information about the whereabouts of the countless victims. My father died in a concentration camp, and I was told by the prosecuting authority almost twenty years later that he had been rehabilitated. Yes, millions of the dead were rehabilitated.

Let us visit the palace of the Kremlin. Built in 1447, it has been altered many times, making it ever more magnificent. It was the architect Thone who built it in the *empire* style as we see it today. The visitor is immediately captivated by the marble columns of the entrance hall, the crystal vases eight feet high, the broad granite staircase, the large painting of the 'Battle of the Field of Snipe'.* From here one enters St. George's Hall, one of the largest rooms in the world. It's name derives from the Cross of St. George, an order instituted by Catherine II as an honour of the highest military distinction. The mirror-like floor, marble and gold walls and colonnades, the bronze chandeliers, the carvings decorating the columns representing Russia's glorious victories, with the gilt inscriptions of the names of famous regiments and knights of the order of St. George; all this splendour is enough to blind the innumerable guests at those great receptions to which ordinary people are almost never asked. Here the 'élite' assembles to celebrate its 'victories', or to decorate the guests with medals. In the adjoining Alexander and Andrey Hall, where the sessions of the highest Soviets are held, but also congresses of Writers' Guilds and those of the musicians and interpretative arts, there has been no lack of propaganda, lies and diatribes. Is there anything the Russian people have not been promised? To outstrip America, to reap record harvests, the Communist Paradise....

In the beautiful Yekaterina and Vladimir rooms which the Tsarinas once used for large receptions, nobody now holds meetings. It may be for this reason that their splendid furniture, their columns of malachite and the crystal chandeliers, the tenderly wrought little tables with inlays of silver and ivory, have preserved not only the taste of past grandeur, but also a certain mysterious atmosphere. Where life once bubbled over, the shadows of the past seem to whisper to each other today. This feeling grows in the chapel of the Tsarinas and the Golden Chamber. In the echoing silence I make my way into the vestibule with its ancient frescoes, and through the white stone portal into the reception hall where Peter the Great celebrated his victory over the Swedes at Poltava. For a long time I stand before Semyon Ushakov's wonderful wall paintings.

From here one enters the Terem (the Tartar name for the women's quarters). This four-storey building with its beautiful frescoes and ornate furniture is also rich with historical association. The last inhabitant of the top storey was the Tsarevitch Alexey who was condemned to death for his part in the Boyar revolt against Peter's reforms. The Boyars wanted to elevate Peter's son, this 'most Christian of successors' to the throne after Peter's downfall.

There is a little belvedere tower on the Terem which commands a wide view of Moscow. It is said that here Pushkin wrote *Boris Godunov*. In the three chapels of the Terem the Tsars prayed to the Almighty to have their sins forgiven, and prayed as well, no doubt, for success in their military campaigns. The collection of weapons in the armoury is a reminder of this.

When one leaves this building one is confronted by the 'Tsar Cannon' which weighs 40 tons. This and the 'Tsar Bell' are of impressive size. In the Patriarch's

Page 33:
Red Square, which runs along the eastern boundary of the Kremlin, has always been called thus, for it is considered the most beautiful square in Moscow, and in Russian the words for 'red' and 'beautiful' have the same root.
We see on the right the Nikolskaya Tower and the Senate Tower; in the centre of the picture the Spasskaya Tower with the Kremlin clock and red star.

Page 34:
In the centre of Red Square stands the Lenin Mausoleum which is visited by thousands of people every day. They wait patiently in long queues. In the left background stands the Cathedral of St. Basil which was built at the time of Ivan the Terrible, between 1554 and 1560. It is considered one of the most 'grandiose' buildings of Russian church architecture. In the left foreground the façade of the department store Gum can be seen.

Page 35:
Young guards in front of the Lenin Mausoleum.

* This was fought in 1380, when Prince Dmitry was victorious over the Tartars.

Palace behind the armoury, which today stands empty, the upper clergy once lived, and they prayed in the Cathedral of the Twelve Apostles which adjoins the palace, a Byzantine church of the 17th century. In modern Moscow the churches, whether Old Russian or Baroque, have been stripped of their function, just as the inhabitants have lost their chance to live a free life. When I went to see the old Moscow churches and houses I often went as to a rendezvous with a young girl, excited, in a hurry—and afraid I might not see them again. For there is little guarantee that Moscow's forty churches will survive when four hundred are gone. Nor has the spiritual Church fared any better. Suppressed until the war in 1941, the Church has since come to an arrangement with the State. But when a priest tries to really guide his flock, when his sermons are too full of the Christian spirit, if he does not praise those in power, he will soon find himself out of office or transferred to some sparsely inhabited region.

Let us leave the Kremlin and enter Red Square. There is an old custom that school-leavers should come to Red Square in June to await the sunrise. They mostly go down to the Moskva where the green of the trees seems gilded from within and sparkles in the light. They walk along the mile of the Kremlin wall, and some remain standing by one of the towers, swearing eternal love or friendship, and promising to serve truth and justice.

The Cathedral of St. Basil in Red Square (it is also called the Pokrovsky, Intercession, Church) is particularly enchanting at sunset. And on still evenings one longs in vain for the soft ringing of its bells. But the eye rejoices at this unique building of which the French poet Theophile Gautier said: 'This is the most original building in the world—it resembles no other, and cannot be attributed to any known style.'

This mighty building was begun in 1552 at the order of Ivan the Terrible. It commemorates the subjugation of the Tartar states of Kazan and Astrakhan. Its architects, Barmin and Postnik, succeeded in creating a unique masterpiece. The cathedral is cruciform, the arms of the cross pointing east and west, north and south, as if the peoples of the whole world wished to summon up unity. The building consists of eight chapels around a central altar. It is crowned by twelve domes with golden crosses at each apex. Each dome has its individual decoration, fluted spirals which seem to flow on eternally, shining in brightly-coloured ceramics. Inside there are wonderful frescoes and icons. Blessèd the Christian soul that can sing God's praises in such a place. But today it is desecrated, the cathedral is a museum.

After the Kremlin fortress had been built all sorts of merchants began to live around it. Warehouses and stalls were opened where all manner of goods were for sale: flax and furs, hardware, paints, leather and cloth, as well as all kinds of foodstuffs. Even Peter the Great's omnipotent minister Menshikov once sold pies in Red Square. To protect this growing community of merchants from enemy attack, it was decided to build a wall around the new settlement. Because of its great length (it was also much stronger than the Kremlin wall), the Muscovites called it the 'Chinese Wall' and the district it surrounded was called Chinatown. Today this would correspond to the district within the radius of Nikolskaya Street, Varvarka and Ilynska with their small side streets as far as Lubyanka and Solyanka Square. This wall was pulled down and only a few sections of it remain, such as those on 41

Pages 36/37:
View from Red Square
over Moscow at night.
In the centre,
the Cathedral of St. Basil;
on the right the
Spasskaya Tower with
its famous carillon.
Beyond the Moskva,
in the background, stands
the Hotel Ukraine
built in the Fifties.
The conglomeration
of old and new buildings
gives the city an unexpected
fascination when seen
at night.

Page 38:
View from the window
of the Hotel Metropole
towards the 'Grand Theatre'
built in 1821 in classical
style, and known
as the Bolshoy Theatre.
To the right lies the
'Little Theatre' built at
the same time.

Page 39:
Gorky Street which leads
to Red Square is one
of the busiest streets
in Moscow.

Page 40:
The Kremlin in evening
light. In the foreground
the 300-foot high
Ivan Veliky clock Tower;
in the background
the domes of the Cathedral
of the Twelve Apostles.

both sides of the Tretyakovsky passage and in Revolution Square. Without the wall it seems very cheerless, for the Muscovites had been used to rummaging in the stalls and boxes of the second-hand dealers, who had their sites there since old times. The Parisians too would miss their second hand stalls! And there weren't even any good books any more.... Books are connected in another way with Chinatown since, in the old days, this was not only a trading centre but also a centre of Russian education. To this day the building of Moscow's first High School, the Slavonic-Greek-Latin Academy, where the great scholar, philosopher and poet Mikhail Lomonossov studied, stands in Nikolskaya Street.

Not far from here stood the first Russian printing press, built by the founder of Russia's printing craft, Ivan Fyodorov. Only the 'House of the Press Corrector' is still there. Towards the end of the last century Chinatown changed from a centre of education to Moscow's 'City', with offices and warehouses, banks and the bourse. The wealth of the Moscovite merchants increased constantly. The celebrated restaurant, the 'Slavonic Bazaar', was opened in Nikolskaya Street. In 1966 it was reopened after being closed for forty years. Its great specialities were sterlet soup, open pies filled with fish, sour sturgeon soup, and boiled meat peasant-style, which was brought to the table in the pan on a small cast-iron stove. Vodka flowed freely, the chorus girls bathed in champagne, cigars were lit with hundred-rouble notes, and Venetian mirrors were broken. After midnight one drove to the 'Yar' or 'Strelna' on the edge of the city, to the Khodunka in what is today Leningrad Avenue. Today the officers of the Shokuvsky Academy of the Air Force have their mess in the 'Strelna', and the restaurant 'Sovietsky' is where the 'Yar' was and where a famous gipsy choir used to appear.

From Lyubyanskaya Square I walk to the Kitaisky-Proyesd which is now called Serov-Proyesd. The first thing I see is the huge building of the Polytechnical Museum. A host of memories come back to me at the sight of it. The Twenties... Enormous placards on the façade of the Polytechnical Museum screaming in yellow letters: 'Tonight, Futurist Evening! Vladimir Mayakovsky reads his poem: *The Cloud in Trousers.*'

Then the Old Square. At the edge of a small green square stands the monument of the victory over the Turks at Plevna. On the right one can just see through the Nikitin cul-de-sac a little church (the Ushakov Museum of today), small and shy like a little old woman lost in the huge Square. A few yards further on the wide Pryamikov Square opens out, full of the atmosphere of the old 'Holy Russia'. Here, behind a crumbling fortress-like wall, lies the old Andronyevsky Monastery. I walk through a heavy stone archway, which has sunk a little in the course of time, and am confronted by one of Moscow's oldest churches, the Church of the Redeemer. The famous artist Andrey Rublev spent a large part of his life at this monastery and decorated the church with many frescoes.

I continue my peregrinations in search of the old Russian Moscow and look with pleasure at the long, low building of the 'Noblemen's Club', now Trade Union House, built in the classical style by the gifted Russian architect Kazakov. The interior is especially surprising. Two rows of marble columns crowned by Corinthian capitals divide the choir from the middle section of the hall. Two rows of ornate crystal chandeliers hang between.

Page 43:
The Lenin Mountains beside the Moskva. They used to be called Sperlings Mountains, and it is from here that Napoleon is said to have caught his first sight of Moscow. With the parks that have been laid out here, they make a popular recreation centre.

Page 44:
An open-air boxing match in front of the exhibition pavilion in the grounds of the permanent Agricultural Exhibition.

Page 45:
In 1909 the department store Gum was built in pseudo-Windsor style. It is approximately 800 feet long and its depth is about 280 feet. It is the show window of the whole of Russian production, and is visited daily by over a hundred thousand people.

Pages 46/47:
Playing chess is a national passion. Russian youth is fascinated by jazz and beat music. The Metro is built on a large scale and the Muscovites have taken it to their hearts.

Pages 48/49:
Lenin Avenue, about 120 feet wide and three miles long, is one of Moscow's busiest arterial roads. On the night between the 5th and 6th of December 1941 the Siberian Regiment marched along it on their way to the decisive battle for Moscow which, as it turned out, decided the outcome of the war.

СОЮЗ СОВЕТСКИХ СОЦИАЛИСТИЧЕСКИХ РЕСПУБЛИК

Kazakov was one of many important Russian architects of the last century. All his Moscow buildings are true masterpieces: the Hall of Columns where Pushkin danced, the former English Club where the poet was often a guest, and the old residence of the Governor of Moscow, where the Moscow City Soviet has its offices.

Moscow's oldest street and its main street, Tverskaya (Gorky Street) has changed more and more in the last few years. Only the former English Club in the palace of Count Rasumovsky, the famous delicatessen shop Yelissyev, the City Soviet, and the White Russian Station remind one of the old Moscow.

But let us move to another part of the old city. There, on a high green hill, stands a remarkable building erected in the Renaissance style by Bashenov in 1786. Originally it served as the residence of a certain Pashkov, but today it serves the whole population. It houses the Lenin State Public Library, one of the largest libraries in the world. It holds not only Russian journals and books, but also those from other countries, more than twenty-five million volumes. There is room for seven thousand readers in the twenty reading rooms.

Further along, in Volkhonka Street stands the Pushkin Museum of West European painting and sculpture. It houses a distinguished collection of French impressionist paintings, and paintings by Matisse, Picasso and Salvador Dali.

Almost all museums in the Soviet Union owe their origins to private initiative. The Tretyakov Art Gallery, for example, was built up from purchases of merchants, men whom the Soviet ideologists would apostrophize as 'fat-bellied bloodsuckers', just as the aristocracy is today represented as the exploiters of feudalism. But at least they created a rich and important culture and employed huge sums to embellish the country. The merchant Pavel Tretyakov built a large addition on to his house in 1871 to hold his treasures. From 1881 the gallery was open to the public and later Tretyakov gave it to the City of Moscow.

Today about forty thousand paintings and sculptures are exhibited in the fifty rooms. True, one looks in vain for some of the works acquired by Tretyakov, they have vanished, since they do not comply with the ideology of the present regime. (Russians are not allowed, for example, to look at the more recent paintings of Marc Chagall who emigrated from Russia.)

I instinctively compare all this splendour with the poverty of present-day Soviet life, and think of the close connection between moral and aesthetic culture. Have the Soviet people sunk so low compared with the Russians of the past, because their life is so unlovely? Their childhood and youth is spent not in palaces and great churches, but in wretched and overcrowded bed-sitting rooms. They have no homes of their own, no holy days, nothing mysterious remains, nothing to stimulate the imagination. Romanticism is rejected, art has become handicraft, physical love a functional appetite, Romeo and Juliet paltry clowns' masks.

It is not difficult to understand, therefore, that one is for ever remembering the old Russia, not simply to mourn the 'good old days', but because the old and the genuine have not been allowed to develop organically, and because they threaten to perish in the unhappy, politically co-ordinated present.

I shall never cease to admire the masterpieces of Russian church architecture. The 17th century church of the Miraculous Nikolay in Khamovniky (in Tolstoy

Street) is a fairytale palace. Its five onion domes, covered in coloured glass tiles, the strange mosaics and the emerald and gold painted domes and side naves, give the impression of a decorative stage set. This is heightened when, in the summer, the hill on which the church stands is covered with brilliantly green grass and yellow dandelions and buttercups.

I love to walk along Pretshistenka Street (today called Krapotkin Street). Not a single new house disturbs its harmony. One might be standing in the 19th century. The 'Scientists House', a Russian baroque building with Corinthian columns, seems to invite one to enter its twilight halls, and to listen to symphony concerts and outstanding soloists. Here one can listen to old ballads sung by the young singer Anna Kareva, to the enchanted playing of the world-famous pianist Svatoslav Richter, or to Italian arias and the wonderful voice of Goar Gasparian.

I walk along Vorovskaya Street. In the past, when it was called Povarskaya, only aristocrats lived here. But though the inhabitants have changed, it has not become a typical Soviet street. There are many foreign embassies along here. At the end of the street, near Kudrinskaya Square, two old buildings belong to the Writers' Union. Leo Tolstoy used one of them in *War and Peace* as the house of Count Rostov. I have spent many days there. It is strange, but the atmosphere of empty propaganda and bureaucracy which prevails there seems to have changed even the outward appearance of these buildings. It is difficult to imagine that Natasha Rostov danced the cotillion with Count Andrey Bolkonsky in this ballroom where for the last decades writers have indulged in so much opportunistic talk.

Moscow has grown far in all directions, especially to the south-west. Fili, Kunzevo, Masilovo, Rublovo, Kaftanovo, Tcheryomushky and many other villages have become Moscow streets. Hundreds of thousands of provincials have become, more or less, Muscovites, for today one cannot speak of a uniformity in population any more than of a uniform architecture.

Among many insignificant buildings in Kirov Street (it used to be called Myasnitskaya), one house stands out. It is number 27, built in 1780. How elegant is its round balcony with Doric columns! Stepping back a few paces from the Myasnizky Gate one can glimpse a multi-storey building in the same street which seems to be made completely of glass, resting on concrete pillars. It is strange, but despite its size, this giant gives an impression of floating lightness. This house was built by Le Corbusier in collaboration with the talented Russian Kolli.

Kalanchovskaya Square which we approach from the Myasnitskaya presents a strange collection of old edifices. Yaroslav Station with its bright paintings, its mosaics, frescoes and coloured ceramic tiles seems to have been transplanted from some Russian myth. Kazan Station repeats in many of its motifs the Kazan Kremlin. The classical Petersburg Station in Moscow seems to be a twin of the Moscow Station in Petersburg. These two were the first Russian railway stations. The whole complex does not remind one of European railway stations, but has an oriental appearance spoilt only by the twenty-two-storey Hotel Leningrad rising like a monstrous giant in the background.

Crossing the wide Russakovskaya Street, we arrive in the beautiful Sokolniki park, and from there we go to the former village of Preobrashenskoye, where the young Peter held his military manoeuvres and formed the famous Preobrashensky

On 22nd June 1812 Napoleon was ready to throw his six hundred thousand strong 'Grand Army' against Moscow. The bloody battle of Borodino had made access to Moscow possible, and on 14th September it was occupied. The following day fire broke out in all parts of Moscow, and this raged for five days and destroyed almost the whole

Guard regiment. There is plenty to admire in this part of Moscow, especially for those interested in antiquities: the Church of the Prophet Elias (who, to judge by the number of churches dedicated to him, was especially venerated by the Muscovites), the ruins of the Nikolayevsky Monastery, and the Preobrashenskoy cemetery and its church, where services are still held according to the ritual of the Old Believers.

In another district of Moscow, in the direction of Bogdan-Khmelnitsky Street, I pause for a long time near the Prkrovsky Gate, arrested by unhappy memories. The Cathedral of the Assumption once stood here, a Russian baroque building. Its noble form, the thirteen domes and the tentlike clocktower, filled Napoleon with such enthusiasm that he commanded it should be especially protected from fire. In this way it escaped destruction by the enemy, but the Communists did not spare it. This marvel of architecture was pulled down because the square had to be enlarged.

Wherever I look in Moscow I find small corners where Russia's spirit and greatness shows itself. In Podmoskovy there is still a group of houses which emanates an intensity of feeling similar to that at Yasnaya Polyana where the old magician Tolstoy worked. People from all over the world called him 'the conscience of mankind' and came to the quiet, white manor house to listen to his words. And today, half a century after his death, thousands of pilgrims make their way to the little station of Astapovo and to Yasnaya Polyana to visit Tolstoy's grave where, so says an old family tradition, a magic wand lies buried which could free mankind from violence and suffering.

But back to Moscow, to the Moskva. The river has become more beautiful since part of the waters of the Volga flow into it. It is broader, and deeper, the water is ruffled into silver waves and beats against the stone banks or on the tall piers of the bridges which are taller now, to let the hugest ships through. For Moscow is, today, connected with five northern and southern seas by the White Sea canal, the Baltic canal, the Moscow canal, and the Volga-Don canal.

On the left bank of the Moskva lies Zamoskvorechy. After the foundation of the Kremlin and the White City, many merchants who supplied the court settled here. The warehouses were filled with all kinds of goods, both Russian and from abroad. Here the trade route to the Volga region and to the Crimea began. Much was brought to Moscow: precious stones from the Urals, copper and ironwork, Siberian furs, wax, honey, flax and hemp, carpets. The merchants grew rich. Their warehouses were protected by the Danilovsky and Donskoy monastery fortresses, the soldiers of the Tsarist guard defended their properties. In the 18th century the merchants began to build splendid houses which rivalled the palaces of the Boyars. There sat those *titushi* with their corpulent wives behind a huge, pot-bellied samovar, surrounded by countless retainers, quaffing twenty glasses of tea one after another, eating meat or fish pies, and praying to God.

Zamoskvorechy, as it is immortalized in Ostrovsky's plays, and as it was presented on the stage of the Little Theatre, belongs to the past. The freedom of the merchants came to an end. Nowadays the families of many Soviet employees are crammed into the large flats. 'Ring twelve times for Ivanov.' Such notices are not unusual. **57**

city. Because of this fire it became impossible for Napoleon to winter there with his army and to force Alexander I to the conference table. On 19th October Napoleon gave the order to retreat. This 'scorched earth policy' saved Russia and was the prelude to the fall of Napoleon. (Contemporary Russian woodcutting.)

Much building goes on in Zamoskvorechy, and haughty neo-classicism is replaced by modern buildings erected from prefabricated sections.

Moscow can be proud of its parks. Sokolniki, Ostankino, the Ismaylovsky and the Kusminsky parks, these are great green expanses with centuries-old oaks and birches, beautiful lawns and meadows, ponds and shady avenues. Here half a million Moscovites can relax from May to September.

The park of Ostankino, formerly the estate of Count Sheremetyev, covers two and a half thousand acres. In it stand the pavilions of the 'Exhibition of the Advances in Political Economy'. To this day a 'Volga' automobile is on exhibition here of which the Muscovites tell the following story. When the then Vice-President Richard Nixon came to Moscow, he was offered a 'Volga' for his use, and he said, pleased: 'The moment I get into this car I feel twenty years younger. We built cars like this exactly twenty years ago.'

Let us climb the Sperlings Mountains. Their venerable old name was changed to Lenin Mountains by those now in power. From their heights one has a splendid view of Moscow, the Kremlin can be seen, Zamoskvorechy, Gorky park, the stadium in Luzniki, Novodevichy monastery, the skyscrapers. In the most beautiful part of the Sperlings Mountains, that spot from which Napoleon first saw Moscow on 14th September 1812, stands Moscow University, built during Stalin's time, looking ostentatious. The whole University complex functions as a student city. The main building has thirty-two storeys and is approximately seven hundred feet high to the top of the tower, which carries a red star. This building contains the central administration of the University and the offices of the Chancellor, and also has in it a students' restaurant, library, swimming-pool, cinema, bookshop, etc. About six thousand rooms are reserved as living quarters for the students. But since around thirty thousand students, including many foreigners, are registered there, most of them have to live elsewhere. To get into the University, the young people have to pass a school certificate examination after ten years at school.

The entrance examinations, which correspond to the West European matriculation, are very hard. Despite this, the Soviet Union has two million university students. By and large the students work hard and with perseverance. If a student's performance deteriorates he is immediately sent down from the university and is then fitted into the industrial work structure. It is characteristic of the spirit of the student body that most students are interested in science and research, but, to the disappointment of the regime, less interested in politics and in the party and the problems of Marxism-Leninism. Their attitude is apolitical.

Young people in Moscow know where to look for the truth, and they will risk their life to bring truth back again. The cultural and spiritual life of Moscow, this living reciprocity between metropolis and provinces, will prove important for the future of Russia.

MOSCOW
DEMONSTRATES
POWER

Page 59:
On the 1st of May each year hundreds of thousands of Soviet citizens march across Red Square to demonstrate the achievements of the Social Revolution.

Pages 60/61:
On each anniversary of the outbreak of the October Revolution of 1917 a large military parade is held in Red Square to demonstrate Russia's military strength. This is also supposed to show the peaceful intentions of the regime and to frighten those who plan revenge.

The Window to the West

The window that Peter the Great opened towards the West was slammed and barricaded fifty years ago. Occasionally just a crack opens and allows the West a glance at wonderful treasures. But nobody can look out. I have spent my whole life in Russia, and I know the opalescent windows and concealing curtains from the inside.

Petersburg, capital throughout two centuries, became the focal point of the best forces of the Russian people. Here one learned what was worth learning from the West, and the city became a symbol for a Russia open to Western progress.

Petersburg has a most distinctive character, and this may account for its reputation as one of the most beautiful cities in the world. From the very beginning it was built to a rigid artistic plan, not like Moscow, chaotically. Peter the Great was indefatigable in providing for the education of architects, sending young people to study abroad, and inviting foreign architects to Russia. Thanks to the admirable collaboration of talented architects such as Rossi, Pastrelli, Quarenghi, Trezzini, Italians for whom Russia became a second home, and of the Russian architects Semzov, Korobov, Voronikhin, this miracle of a city was created. They all worked to a plan which had been drawn up in 1737 by the St. Petersburg building commission, with the gifted city planner Yeroshkin at its head.

Petersburg—Venice of the North! The granite banks of the Neva and the innumerable canals are wonderful in their strict simplicity and stateliness. One cannot but remember Pushkin's words when he speaks of the 'royal Neva flowing between the rich stone buildings of harmonious splendour'. The hundreds of bridges of Petersburg, an epic of stone and metal, were all created by great Russian masters. Every one of the six hundred bridges is different, the big ones full of dignity, lying like a lace veil over the shoulders of the Neva, the small, humpbacked bridges full of a homely, intimate magic. Here Orlov's riders galloped over the quays and bridges, hoofs clattering over the pavements of hexagonal wood blocks. Here young aristocrats and famous Petersburg beauties hurried to banquets and court receptions. Today all this is lost and forgotten. Today one hears the rumbling of overcrowded trams. There are queues in front of the shops, people with gloomy, tired faces. Lermontov comes to mind:

Page 62:
A ceremonial corps
of drummers traditionally
concludes the military parade
in Red Square.

... with cold attention you look around—
How comical and stupid a joke is this life!

63

The greatest poets have sung of Petersburg. On the banks of the Neva, Dostoevsky, in the sleepless white nights, created his immortal heroes, and revealed the terrible abyss of unbelievable passions. In Petersburg, Alexander Blok saw the *Terrible World,* here he had his memorable meeting with *The Unknown,* his twelve Red Guards walked the nocturnal Prospects through the snowy night during the revolution. Nikolay Agnivzev wrote the verses which are dedicated to Petersburg's hard and hungry time at the beginning of the Twenties:

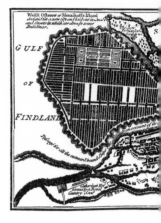

> Oh, Petersburg—how very simply
> Your time approaches an untimely end!
> Oh bring some food for the Troizky bridge!
> To the Winter Palace carry bread!
> . . . . .
> Before a single penny bun
> St. Petersburg has bent its knee.

*Town plan
of Petersburg*

During the Second World War it was mainly the poets and painters who kept up the morale of the people, patiently enduring the terrible times at home. Andrey Bely's almost forgotten novel *Petersburg* did homage to the beautiful city on the Neva.

For some mysterious reason, all streets in Petersburg lead to the Neva. It is natural to go first to the Dvorzovaya embankment, to the Senate Square and the bronze horseman, famous monument to Peter the Great. Here on the stone flags the unfortunate Paul I liked to do riding tricks. He had had the greatest difficulty in getting to power, his mother, Catherine, was much too much alive, and when he finally managed it, he could not enjoy his power. His own son deprived him of his crown and of his life. It was here that, in March 1881, the fate of Alexander II was decided by a shot fired by the terrorist Solovyov, and there stand the Alexander colums, in memory of Alexander I's victory over Napoleon. This strange Tsar, who was not quite of this world, a mystic, Freemason and Liberal, at the same time the protector of a chief of police, managed to be neither the servant of God, nor the pupil of the devil, and departed this life in very strange circumstances. To this day there is a legend that it was not the Tsar who was buried at Taganrog, but a common soldier, while Alexander wandered about Russia as Starez Fyodor Kumitch, a haversack over his shoulder, begging for alms. All the Russian Tsars were eccentrics. While they dreamed of solid power, they weakened it by their moods and caprices, and often lost it altogether here, on this very square, for it was from here that the last Tsar of all was taken to Sverdlovsk, exile and death.

The Winter Palace stands almost unprotected in this large square. It leans against the Hermitage as if seeking shelter. The Hermitage really consists of three buildings, the small, the old, and the new. Together they form a great triangle, and it seems as if the whole Russian State stood to attention on the bank of the Neva. At the time of Peter, the house of Apraxin, a well-known aristocrat, stood on this spot, but it was demolished by order of the Tsarina Anna. Then the Winter Palace was built from a plan by Rastrelli.

I have always thought of this palace as an immense treasure-chest, ornamented with a mass of decorations and capricious adornments. Imagine: this building alone

64

*This engraving, after a
painting by Benjamin Paiter,
shows the
Petersburg Palace Bridge
at the beginning
of the 19th century.
In the background one can
recognize the Isaacs
Cathedral; on the left of it
stands the Admiralty, easily
recognizable by its 'needle'.*

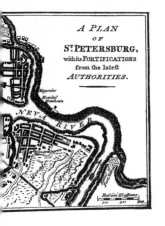

has one hundred and seventy-six antique statues, with as many amphorae in between, the ledges decorated with masks and lions heads. The arches of the three gates in the main façade rest on white marble columns. The gate of the New Hermitage is supported by caryatids nineteen feet high. The interior is equally splendid: stairs of marble from Carrara where foreign ambassadors once mounted to the throne room, panelling in different kinds of precious woods with beautiful inlays. In the malachite hall the precious stones from the Urals shine as splendidly as in a fairy-tale. The enormous complex of buildings surpasses in splendour the Louvre, Versailles or Westminster. In its one thousand five hundred rooms more than two million pictures and sculptures are kept, masterpieces from all countries and all times.

The city began with the building of the Peter-and-Paul fortress. The Peter-and-Paul Cathedral gave it its name. Its four-part clock tower is particularly beautiful; rising above the western section of the church, it has a lovely gold spire which can be seen from far off. It is crowned by a flying angel with the infant Jesus, the golden flag on that great Baltic vessel Petersburg. To give his new capital greater importance, Peter demanded that the tower should be higher than that of the Kremlin. And in fact the approximately three hundred and thirty-foot high spire of the Peter-and-Paul Cathedral is a little higher than the clock tower of the Kremlin. The interior of the cathedral matches its airy yet noble exterior. There is a beautiful gilded wooden iconostasis made by Moscow masters.

The Summer Palace of the Tsars stands in the summer gardens which were laid out at the same time as most of Petersburg. Peter concerned himself personally with its layout, and several Russian architects and the best gardeners assisted Le Blond, who had been especially invited to come from France. They created a wonderful park with a large orangery and a gallery, an exotically painted grotto, an aviary for rare birds, and more than fifty fountains with allegorical sculptures. The monument to the famous poet of fables, 'Papa Krylov' as the children call him, is an especial favourite.

When one strolls along the banks of the Neva, the largest of the islands of the Petersburg archipelago, the Vasilyevsky Island, is often in sight. Here lived Alexander Menshikov, first governor-general of Petersburg and favourite of the Tsar. Nearby stands the administrative building designed by Trezzini and known as the 'Twelve Colleges'. Today it is the University where eminent scholars and writers have studied.

Radiant, glorious Petersburg! Wherever one looks there are magnificent views and unique buildings.

Before me stand the buildings of the Senate and the Synod, the work of Carlo Rossi, who, like Rastrelli, bound his fate to that of Russia. Opposite the Winter Palace rises the building of the General Staff, also a work of Rossi's. It is built in *empire* style in the form of a horseshoe of white stone, and an archway leads through it to the Nevski Prospect. Its ornate façade is more than five hundred yards long. The world-famous triumphal arch in front of it dominates the square with its enormous victory chariot, its six horses seeming to strain towards the Winter Palace. In the chariot itself stands the Goddess of Glory, the State insignia in her hand. It was through this arch that victorious Russian troups used to parade.

And here is the Admiralty. This great work by Zakharov is the very soul of the northern capital and epitomizes the power of the Russian State. From whichever 65 direction one approaches Petersburg, the first thing one sees is the golden needle of the Admiralty. It is unforgettable. Pushkin, Petersburg's great poet, wrote:

> When in my room, awakened from my dreams,
> I write or read without a lamp or light,
> Beyond my window-sill the city bright
> Lies like an august picture,
> And from the distant Admiralty
> The needle's gleaming gold salutes me...

This gigantic building is monumental and somehow weightless at the same time. The middle part forms a large cube with a high, much subdivided tower. Its somewhat smaller second storey and its side wings are surrounded by Ionic columns. Above this rises a huge glass cupola which ends in the golden needle, crowned by a golden ship. This rises to about two hundred feet above the ground.

The most grandiose church in the city is the Isaacs Cathedral which fits harmoniously into the historical centre of Petersburg. Its huge gilt dome serves, as does the Admiralty needle and the Peter-and-Paul Cathedral, as a main point of orientation in the city. The Isaacs Cathedral dazzles the onlooker not only with its shining dome, but also with its disconcerting masses of gold, marble and sculptures, all of which seem to symbolize the greatness, the wealth and the power of a people who could build such a church, where twelve thousand people might pray to God—if they were allowed to.

The Isaakievskaya Square is framed on two sides by modest *empire* buildings, used today as Departments of Agriculture and State Ownership. In the middle of the square stands the equestrian statue of Nicholas I.

Beyond this square, on the bank of the Moika, stands house number 12. Here Pushkin lived. He died of a mortal wound received in a duel which had been forced on him. This memory brings with it a bitter thought: how much have we Russians achieved, great art, great poetry, churches, palaces. Yet how little of it have we been able to preserve. We have been unable to protect our great poets, we have lost many marvellous churches, we have left Russia's glory to a godless regime which overwhelms with praise creators of 'non-art', as Alberto Moravia expressed it.

A little further along the Moika is the Field of Mars. Originally this was called the 'Pleasure Gardens' after the garden festivals and fireworks displays which took place there. Since the beginning of the last century it has been used for military parades, and its name was changed accordingly. In 1801 the sculptor Kolovsky erected a monument to the brilliant commander-in-chief Suvorov which stands here.

The historical centre of Petersburg seems inexhaustible. I went there so often, yet every time I was surprised by new impressions and unexpected discoveries.

From the Siny bridge I look at Theatre Square where, in 1730, the first Petersburg theatre was built. In 1886 the Marinsky Theatre was opened, and the old building was converted to accommodate the Conservatoire, where some of the great Russian composers, Tchaikovsky, Rimsky-Korsakov, Glazunov and Lyadov studied. There are monuments to Glinka and Rimsky-Korsakov outside the Conservatory.

Page 67:
Characteristic picture of the 'Venice of the North'. Part of the Moika bank with the Cathedral of the Resurrection built on the spot where Tsar Alexander II was assassinated.

Page 68:
Monument of Peter the Great, popularly known as the 'Bronze Horseman'.

Page 69:
The Hermitage, one of the most famous museums in the world. It holds incomparable masterpieces of Western art, paintings by Fra Angelico, Leonardo da Vinci, Michelangelo, Raphael, Titian, Giorgione, Veronese, Tiepolo.... The collection of twenty-five works by Rembrandt is world-famous. French painting is represented by great works from Poussin to Picasso.

Pages 70/71:
The Summer Garden, which stretches over thirty-eight acres, is one of Leningrad's most beautiful parks. Peter I had it laid out in the Dutch and French style. It has grottoes, ponds, fountains and waterfalls. In the shady avenue of limes many statues by Italian masters of the 18th century stand, and they give this park a particularly pleasant character.

The fame of the Russian ballet was born at the Marinsky Theatre, and it has grown ever since. For two hundred years our ballerinas and dancers have enchanted the world. The fame of Anna Pavlova or Galina Ulanova will never fade. Yet new stars have already appeared on this Olympus of the theatre: Maya Plisezkaya, Fedoseyeva, Strutskova, Bovt, and the young Natasha Bessmertnova. Balletomanes all over the world are delighted by their grace and art. The ballet masters Sergeyev, Skharov, Lavronsky and Vayonen are worthy pupils of their teachers Petipa, Nishinsky, Diaghilev, Fokine and Ivanov. The Moiseyev Ensemble which specializes in character dancing, and the Berioska Ensemble under the direction of Nadeshnida are popular all over the world. Our ballets are not welcomed as emissaries of Socialism, but as an expression of truly natural Russian art.

Across the Kiss Bridge I come to the island of New Holland, and here stands the favourite church of everyone in Petersburg, the Preobrashensky Church, built in 1743. Ancient icons in which the faces of the Madonna and Christ, of the saints and angels, have darkened, fill it with an atmosphere of great holiness. Its vaulted ceilings are so enormous that it is difficult to appreciate their frescoes with the naked eye.

All important historical events took place in or around the Nevski Prospect which begins in Dvorzovaya Square. 1812 was the pinnacle of Russia's glory. To celebrate the great victory, the Kazan Cathedral in Petersburg was built, a poem of granite and bronze. I have seen all the famous cathedrals: St. Peter's in Rome, Notre-Dame in Paris, the cathedral of Milan, St. Mark's, St. Paul's in London; but the Kazan Cathedral is the most beautiful. This great work of Voronichin is often compared with St. Peter's. Yet how much more courageous and grandiose is Voronichin's design. While Bernini's colonnades connect the wings of St. Peter's and thus create a circle, here the columns open out like the wings of an eagle, and the Nevski Prospect marches past this saluting base of one hundred and thirty six granite columns with Corinthian capitals, as if all the heroes of that patriotic war were assembled to inspect an army filing past. Indeed, in the niches behind the columns we may observe figures which seem to bless the Russian weapons of defence, portrait sculptures of Prince Vladimir and Alexander Nevski, the Apostle Andrew and John the Baptist. Like the exterior, the interior of the Kazan Cathedral cannot be compared with any other cathedral in the world. If anything, it reminds one of the throne room in the Palace of the Tsars! Monolithic columns with Corinthian capitals of bronze support the stucco-decorated vaulted ceiling. The middle door, ornamented in bronze, is reminiscent of the Ghiberti door of the Baptistry in Florence. The silver iconostasis contains the ancient jewelled icon of the Madonna of Kazan. Today this House of God is another museum.

Strolling along the Nevski Prospect, I remember Gogol's words: 'There is nothing more beautiful than the Nevski Prospect... in this the most lovely of all the streets of our capital, you will find anything that the heart desires.' The Nevski—work of innumerable masters: there stands the old Duma, the old Catholic church of St. Catherine with the grave of the Polish King Stanislas Poniatovski, the Mikhailovsky Palace, the Philharmonic Hall, once the noblemen's club, the Mikhailovsky Theatre, today called the Small Opera House. Here stands the Saltikov-Shchedrin Public Library, the second largest in the Soviet Union, and then the Alexandrinsky Theatre, the 'Alexandrinka' as the people of Petersburg still call the Pushkin Theatre.

Pages 72/73
The legendary Winter Palace, the storming of which by Red Guards on 7th November 1917 ushered in the assumption of power by the Bolsheviks. The palace was built by the Italian architect Rastrelli in the middle of the 18th century. The Alexander column, approximately one hundred feet high, which was erected by Tsar Nicholas I in 1834, stands in this square. It was carved from a single stone.

Page 74:
The 'ships prows', signal towers in Leningrad harbour. Oil was poured into the copper vessels on top of the columns and set alight in celebration.

But sometimes it is the quite ordinary, unobtrusive houses rather than the masterpieces of architecture that move the heart of a Russian as he passes by. On the Nevski, for instance, there is number 68, no different from its neighbours. But Turgenyev, Belinsky and Pissarev lived here, and Dostoevsky, Nekrassov and Bakunin were frequent guests. And a multitude of questions come into my mind when I look up at the windows of number 68. One question outweighs all others: Why did the most outstanding of Russians have to bear so hard a destiny? Yet there is a bitter sweetness about their fate: at least theirs were real lives, full of strife and passion, catastrophe and rapture.

Near the Peter-and-Paul fortress, the bed of the river Neva widens considerably and divides into two arms: the large and the small Neva. The arches of bridges cut across the Petersburg horizon in all directions. Crossing Dvorzovy Bridge, one finds oneself in Pushkin Square, the centre of the so-called Strelka, the favourite promenade for 19th century Petersburg society.

Pushkin Square was formerly Petersburg's most important harbour, the centre of its trade, and the most outstanding architects did their utmost to make this gateway to the capital as magnificent as possible. The most important building of the district, the bourse, or money-market, bears witness to that. According to contemporary witnesses this was the most grandiose Exchange in the whole world. Today it too is a museum. On each side of the Exchange stand two columns decorated with the prows of ships. They remind one of the old custom of celebrating naval victories by erecting triumphal columns, decorated with the prows of enemy ships.

Many of our scientists have studied at the Montaigne Institute, Russia's oldest University. When I think of our great scholars, I remember the generalization put forward by Soviet ideologists that science and religion are enemies. This naïve assertion has become an axiom although it is generally known that many scientists have been religious people. The best example is Pavlov, of whom Russian scholars are so proud. He was a pious Christian all his life.

The Kirovsky Prospect, which leads to the centre of the old town, is a residential street of mansions. At one end stands a house with a façade of ceramic tiles. The ballerina Kshesinskaya, favourite of the last Tsar, lived here like a queen. Then Lenin, of all people, moved into the same house, but he lived in a democratically proletarian style. Today the House is a museum.

Again and again, as I continue my walk, I meet Peter the Great. The massive Ismailov-Troizky Cathedral swims in a veil of haze. Its five azure, star-strewn domes can be seen from afar. Legend has it that this church was built on the spot where Peter the Great first saw his future wife, Catherine I. I have often reflected on the fate of this remarkable woman. Not a few women have sat on the throne, others were mistresses of Kings or Emperors and ruled for a time, but these were princesses. Catherine I, whose real name was Martha, was no Marquise like Madame de Maintenon, but a simple Estonian washer-woman who could barely read or write. When she was made a prisoner after the battle of Narva, the great Menshikov, captivated by her beauty, took her as his concubine. A few days later Peter met her. He learned to appreciate her in quite a different way, recognized her real greatness, and made her his wife and Empress, later his worthy successor. She continued to fight the Boyars' opposition with all her power, but reigned only a short time. She died from an

LENINGRAD

Page 77:
The banks of the Neva
in the cold of winter.
In the background, left,
the Admiralty 'needle';
right, the silhouette of the
St. Isaacs Cathedral.

Page 78:
A room in the Leningrad
'Russian Museum'
which holds a rich collection
of Russian works of art,
from the icons of Rublev
through bourgeois art
of the 19th and early
20th centuries,
up to the much discussed
'social realism' of the
present day.

Page 79:
Peter the Great's
banqueting table
at Peterhof.
(Meissen china.)

Pages 80/81:
The Nevski Prospect,
the main arterial road
of Leningrad.
This splendid street
is about two miles long and
a hundred feet wide.
It traverses the centre
of the city and is flanked
by a great many historical
buildings.

Page 82:
The old Tikhvinskoye
cemetery. Here lie many
famous Russians,
amongst them Glinka,
Mussorgsky, Borodin,
and Tchaikovsky.
Our picture shows the
grave of Dostoevsky.

unknown disease at the height of her powers. However, it seems to me much more likely that the unofficial version of her death is the true one, and that she was 'eliminated' by the Naryshkins or Lopushins. Peter's first wife Yevdokya, who lived in exile in a convent, was a member of the Lopushin family.

Peter the Great's character is most truly reflected by the magnificent Peterhof. This unique piece of architecture has been called the Russian Versailles. Peterhof lies on the shore of the Gulf of Finland. Twenty palaces and pavilions, one hundred and twenty-five fountains, three waterfalls, two hundred statues, all scattered throughout seven parks, make an incomparable complex of splendour. It took almost two centuries of enthusiastic and heroic work by great architects, painters, sculptors, engineers, decorators, woodworkers and other artisans to create it. It was begun after the battle of Poltava and the victory over Sweden.

On a hill in the middle of Peterhof stands its dominating and most important building, the Grand Palace. Its centre part is connected with its wings by glassed-in galleries. These are surmounted by domes, one carrying a cross, the other the Russian arms. The Grand Palace has been reconstructed several times, for the last time after it had been destroyed by the Germans in the Second World War.

One of the finest constructions of Peterhof is the Grand Cascade. This grandiose waterfall runs the whole length of the façade of the Palace. One sees, between the two descending stairs, the five arches of the main grotto. From the forecourt of the grotto, five marble steps lead to a round basin. Into this pool the water cascades, and in the middle stands the world-famous fountain of Samson. Figures of tritons, nymphs and naiads play among the water jets. At night the water, marble and granite are dramatic under spotlights.

From here the 'Avenue of the Fountains' runs right to the mirror-smooth surface of the Gulf of Finland, flanked by Voronikhin's pavilions with their bronze domes and granite lions in their forecourts.

The inhabitants of the Leningrad of today welcome guests from all countries with open arms to their 'Piter', the pet name for their city. No doubt Petersburg will once again become a mediator between East and West. As soon as the bars of this 'window' have been broken, its citizens will carry an open Russian spirit out to the whole world.

Page 83:
Leningrad women paving the streets. The enormous losses of the Second World War forced the women to do even the most arduous men's work. They still do it!

Page 84:
Leningrad harbour. In the background the Admiralty wharf where fine ships are built.

The Community

There are in modern society many kinds of organized groups: the team, kibbutz, confederation. In the Soviet Union everything is collectivized. That is part of the system, but when it is imposed, communal working, eating, living loses its meaning. Collectivism is lifeless, inorganic, and no amount of talk about brotherhood will make it come alive. The results of such forced collective labour have been proved to be poor, and it is well known what the economic results have been.

Yet living as a community is an inborn characteristic of the Russian people. This 'democratic' kind of feeling for life did not depend upon theory, but proved splendidly practical in the life of the peasants as well as in city life.

In the towns it took the form of *vetche* (council, or town assembly) where, as long as six hundred years ago, in the old Princely States, all men assembled to decide upon war or peace. Novgorod was such a town, the 'Great Novgorod' near the lake of Ilmen on the banks of the Volkhov. Today it is a small, quiet provincial town, but once it was the scene of great historical events. In the 12th century, when Moscow was no more than a small settlement, Novgorod was already known as an important trading centre. Goods were brought from all over Russia, and there was a lively trade with Sweden and the German Hanseatic towns. Great Novgorod had to maintain its independence, and it had to defend itself against the Swedes, the Teutonic Knights and the Tartars. At the head of the city stood, like a kind of parliament, the 'Council'. But in 1487 Novgorod was conquered by the Muscovite Prince Ivan III, and though it is not known when the council was suspended, there is no doubt that the 'good old days' were over for Novgorod.

In Novgorod it is not hard to find reminders of ancient times. One meets them at every step. In the centre of the town lies the Kremlin (Detinez) surrounded by 11th-century stone walls, and once inside the Kremlin one's attention is immediately attracted by the remarkable Cathedral of St. Sophia. The bronze Sigun Gate which was taken from the Swedes in 1187, and the Korsun Gate which came from Germany, lend this church a unique dignity. Not far from the Cathedral stands the 'Reception Hall', the former residence of the higher clergy.

There are more than fifty churches and monasteries in Novgorod. The masterpiece of Novgorod church architecture is the 17th-century Snamensky Cathedral with its five noble domes, a gallery and architrave.

Neighbouring Pskov, first heard of in the 8th century, was also a democratic republic like Novgorod. The 'Council' elected two governors who conducted the

The reign of Peter I, the Great (1689 to 1725), was one of the most impressive and grandiose periods of Russian history. He was the first Russian Tsar to visit Western Europe, informing himself in Germany, Holland and England about the state of civilization. The whole of Russia profited from his two-year-long 'Grand Tour' which encouraged him to Europeanize the country, starting a process which has not come to an end to the present day. (Engraving by Houbraken after a painting by Maternovi.)

city's affairs. It was in Pskov that a constitution was first written down, even before the 'Russian Law'.

Pskov lies on the Velikaya. On a spur of the mountains stands its Kremlin, built in the 14th century. One of the finest architectural monuments in Russia is the Cathedral of the Holy Trinity built in the 13th century and still very well preserved. Later, on the advice of the council, an additional system of defence was built. It consists of three parts: the Devmontov city, the middle and the outer city. Its fortified walls are about six miles long.

At the beginning of the 16th century, the schools of Novgorod and Pskov had developed an individual style of architecture and painting. At their head stood the architect Postnikov, designer of the Cathedral of St. Basil in Moscow.

The democratic spirit of the cities of Novgorod and Pskov belongs to the past, and so does the communal spirit of the peasants and village communities. Yet I believe that this spirit still sleeps alongside the will to freedom in the country people. The *mir,* or peasant community, was a style of life congenial to the Russian people. Together they deliberated on peasant affairs in the old 'free times', about harvest or sowing, and until the 16th century the *mir* also functioned as a court of law. Then the rights to freedom were lost to the feudal lords, and not until 1861 did the farming community again have the right to organize and plan its own husbandry. A considerable number of peasants increased their holdings, enlarged their business, and became large-scale farmers. But nobody could leave the farming community and become independent except with the permission of the council. Communal discussion and communal council lie in the Russian blood. And though such debates often delayed decisions, they were superior to the system of total planning. That people had a real feeling of solidarity is shown by the proverb: 'In the *mir* even dying is beautiful.'

One meets the word *mir* in another significant place. In every church service, the choir sings: '*mirom Gospodu pomolimsya*'—'Together let us pray to the Lord'. The brotherhood of man goes back to the brotherhood in faith. The communal 'standing before God' makes that brotherhood grow. But one cannot deify collectivism!

In the Russian Church, in Orthodox belief, the concept of *ssobornosty** is all-embracing and at the same time of primary and fundamental significance. The philosopher Khomyakov called *ssobornosty* 'the soul of Orthodoxy'. It embraces, as Sergey Bulgakov has demonstrated, the council and ecumenical aspect on the one hand, and catholicity on the other hand as the mystical and metaphysical aspects of the *one Church,* a qualitative rather than a quantitative concept which characterizes the Russian Orthodox faith. It is important in this connection to note Khonyakov's statement that Orthodoxy must work against the self-assertion of authority as much as against individualism, and that it embodies 'unanimity', 'synthesis of authority', and 'freedom in that love that unites the faithful'. All this is contained in the concept of *ssobornosty.*

Within such communities the individual personality carries no weight *per se.* Everyone is 'only' a creature of God. Thus one's attitude was the same to everybody, to the tramp, the seeker after truth, the *yurodivy* (Christ's fool)—and to the guest. At all festive meals an extra place was set for the unknown guest who would be welcomed like the wandering Christ himself, a beautiful and profound custom.

* Council, in the widest sense.

87

Pushkin used the *yurodivy* in idealized form in *Boris Godunov*. This feeble-minded creature comes, so says popular belief, as an emissary of God. Since he is dull-witted he has no responsibility, and like the court jester, may tell the truth where normal people remain silent. When he calls to Tsar Boris: 'I see blood on you', he symbolizes the awakening conscience, the voice of God, and thus ushers in the fall of the Tsar.

The *yurodivy* used to appear in small towns and villages. I remember having seen such figures as a child. People tolerated and pitied them as creatures of God with a soul like everybody else. To insult a soul (to 'spit on someone's soul') was the worst one could do to a person. The 'people of God', as they were also called, were tolerated, but they themselves were only interested in the bazaars, in the shopkeepers who might give them a little something to eat, and not in the churches.

Such a figure from the past might well be wandering through an old town called Rostov-Yaroslavsky, a little town itself a relic of the Russian past. It seems as if the whole small, sleepy town on the banks of its lake had been transformed into a jewel casket. Once it was the centre of an autonomous principality, and even carried the proud name of Rostov-Veliky, Great Rostov, but in 1474 it was destroyed by the Tartars and burnt down, and it never regained its former importance. The most interesting building that remains is, of course, the Kremlin which is surrounded by a white-plastered brick wall. Its half-military, half-religious use lends it a strange character. The oldest church in the Kremlin, the Church of the Assumption, was built as early as 1164. For a time the Metropolitan had his residence in Rostov, but when he moved away, many buildings fell into disrepair.

From the banks of the Volga one can admire the ancient town of Yaroslavl. This was once the residence of Yaroslav the Wise, and it is the cradle of the Russian theatre. In 1751 the young merchant Fyodor Volkov, a gifted actor, founded a theatre here.

The city has much to be proud of: its beautiful esplanade on the banks of the Volga, the old park, the museum in the old palace built in the 17th century, the Church of the Transfiguration (1216), the Cathedral of the Ascension, the Church of St. John the Baptist, and the Cathedral of the Prophet Elias which was built with money given by two wealthy burghers, Bonifaz and Joann Sirilin.

Yaroslavl and Rostov also remind me very much of Vladimir and Suzdal. These towns somehow belong together and remain as indestructible monuments of Russia's might and greatness, but also of her communal work and life.

Vladimir lies beside the picturesque little river Klyazma, a tributary of the Moskva. It was founded in 1116 by Vladimir Monomakh, flourished in the 12th century under Prince Andrey Bogolyubsky, and was heavily damaged in the Tartar attack of 1238. But many of its buildings survived, especially the Golden Gate which had been erected in 1164 and was modelled on the Golden Gate of Kiev; also the Cathedral of the Ascension, one of Russia's oldest churches, dating from the beginning of the 12th century. This has wonderful frescoes by Andrey Rublov and Danila Tcherny. There is also the Roshdestvensky monastery, which is said to be the largest in Russia. Nowhere in the world are there as many cathedrals, churches and monasteries as in Vladimir and Suzdal.

Suzdal lies not far from Vladimir, another beautiful old Russian town. Formerly it had fifty churches, twenty monasteries, and a correspondingly active spiritual life.

88

After the Tartar attack of 1238, Suzdal remained devastated for a long time. Not until the 16th century was it rebuilt. Then a whole group of architects, painters and artisans began to reconstruct the Kremlin, the fortifications and towers, the Cathedral of the Nativity, and other churches. At the time of the Polish intervention (1608) and the attacks by the Crimean Tartars (1634) the city was laid waste once more.

Today Suzdal is a dead town, reminiscent of Pompeii. The ruined buildings, only now being partially restored, tell the whole story of Russian architecture.

The monastery of the 'New Jerusalem' on the steep banks of the river Istra looks impressive, and so does the little town of Svenigorod, a little to the south. This too has a well-preserved monastery. Most of the churches of Svenigorod were blown up by the German troops in the Second World War, but the monastery has been partly restored. The Cathedral of the Ascension, which has a remarkably fine pediment and was built in 1393 in the old Novgorod style, has also been preserved. Religious services can still be held there, a sanctioned framework, if only a small one, for *ssobornosty*. This concept is sure to grow again in the hearts of a pious people both in the small old towns and in the big modern cities, and to bring unity once more. The Russian people need this so much, for the last fifty years have undermined people's trust in one another. Instead of a 'synthesis of authority', a minority has wielded arbitrary, cruel power, while the overwhelming majority has suffered and endured. But while Russians live, the will to 'freedom in love' lives with them.

State and Subject

For centuries—until 1861—we, the backward and all too patient Russian peasants, allowed ourselves to live in a degrading state of bondage, and to continue in the twilight of our enormously simple, crude way of life. The landowner tormented, beat and oppressed us. In literature we have innumerable examples of serf and master, though these examples sometimes also show the more human aspect of these relationships, as in Lyesskov for example.

In fact serfdom developed only quite late from the natural conditions of feudalism: the Boyar was bound to furnish his Prince with a certain number of soldiers, and the peasant had to look after the land and pay the Boyar a certain amount of taxes. In the 16th century the law still allowed the Russian peasant to move to another place after the autumn harvest, but in reality this was hardly possible. There were then still trade councils, the *zemsky sobory* in which the peasants had representatives. At the time of the early Romanovs, after the *zemsky sobor* had elected the Tsar Mikhail in 1612, it was, if not a parliamentary institution, at the least the psychological germ of one. The trade council was not, of course, a legislative body but functioned in an advisory capacity. Also, class distinctions were so extreme that it was unable to function as a corporate body.

The Boyars lost their importance as a class at the 'time of the troubles' (at the beginning of the 17th century) and even before this through the endeavours of Ivan the Terrible to root out the enemies inside the State. By creating the *oprikhnina* (dividing the territories of the State in such a way that about half of it was directly subservient to the Tsar), a new class of landowners emerged, and these also became courtiers.

The *Ulosheny* (code of law) of 1649 legalized serfdom. It ordered a census and registration of all people for the sake of the security of the State, and at the same time withdrew from them on all private and State properties the right to choose their domicile, or any semblance of independence. This was a guarantee to the landowners that work would be done, and to the State that the taxes of the peasants, for which the landowners were responsible, would be paid.

When the demands of the State increased, it was the broad mass of this country population which had to bear the brunt. As we have already seen, Peter the Great needed great armies of soldiers and builders. He needed money and still more money to reorganize the army and to build up the fleet, and to carry through the cultural Europeanization. He turned the screw as far as it would go and decreed that the previously privileged peasants of the monasteries should be made equal with the serfs.

In this contemporary woodcut, the horseman is Tsar Ivan IV, surrounded by hangmen, conducting a public execution.

Ivan IV, who occupied the throne as an autocrat from 1547 to 1584, is, in Russian, given the name 'grosny', 'the threatening one', but in the West he is called 'the Terrible'.

He was very gifted, decidedly intellectual, passionately interested in philosophical and theological questions, knew much about literature, was himself an excellent writer, and also composed music. At the same time he was

The situation under Catherine II was particularly unjust. In 1785 she decreed that the nobles had various new rights: no compulsory war service, no taxes, no corporal punishment (!), the right to inherit their titles, legal acknowledgement by the assembly of nobles (which gave them influence in the provincial and regional courts of law). The nobility was thus relieved of all duties towards the sovereign, and the basic balance of the feudal state was destroyed. Catherine's move assured her of the support of the nobility, but intensified pressure on the serfs. The gap between landowner and serf widened. And this was at a time when the universities came under the influence of Voltaire, whose 'natural right' was taught there!

One certainly does not get this impression immediately, but Russia had in fact been a constitutional state ever since the time of Kiev. Let us remember the codices of Yaroslav the Wise, and the decrees of Vladimir Monomakh: true vehicles of justice! Not all later laws were just and humane, and only too often did the lure of autocratic power cause Princes and Tsars to disregard legislation. Peter the Great created his procurators general who were called 'the eyes of the Tsar' and kept him informed of all that went on in the administration and among the people. Nicholas I revived the secret police, creating a third section of the Tsar's private chancellery which functioned not under the law but directly under the Emperor. This institution, though belonging to the capitalist past, if not indeed to feudal times, still enjoys a place in the State in the name of 'Socialism'.... Its efficiency has increased considerably since then. Nicholas I's organization did not prevent such destructive satires as Gogol's *Dead Souls* and *Revisor,* or Saltikov's *Tales of a City* and *Contemporary Idylls*, which were printed and read!

When Alexander I (1801 to 1825) came to power, there arose confidence that his humane and liberal beliefs would lead to a turn for the better. And indeed, the hopes of the élite trained in western conceptions of freedom seemed justified when a number of liberal reforms of civil rights became law. In 1802 the Senate, which had been founded by Peter the Great, became the Supreme Court. The ministries were organized more flexibly. In 1810 a legislative assembly was created, but the executive remained firmly in the hands of the Tsar. And the autocracy fortified itself against internal revolutionary elements after, with the help of the Russian people and the sacrifice of its soldiers, the most modern, seemingly invincible army of Napoleon had been defeated, and the world impressed by the example of Russian power. The military parade before the Tsar in the Place de la Concorde in Paris seems to haunt the West, if only unconsciously, to this day: a free Russia is capable of anything!

The Holy Alliance (the name is significant; Alexander I insisted that it should be used) between Russia, Austria and Prussia in 1815 confirmed the principle of monarchy.

Half a century later Alexander II and his advisors tried to anticipate the threat from the peasant population whose hunger for land grew as fast as their numbers increased. But the Tsar could not instigate land reform without the agreement of the landowners without jeopardizing his throne. Thus the reforms were not only too late but too limited. True, serfdom was abolished, but life did not change for the peasants. When the administrative system resting on the rights of the nobles ceased to function in 1864, the new *semstvo law* came into force. Provinces and districts now elected local administrations in which the representatives of the nobles had, of course, special

a sadist who practised perversions and sexual excesses, arranged mass murders and yet, from time to time, tried to expiate his sins by living a monkish, ascetic life in a monastery. But this did not prevent him from committing new atrocities. His victims were not only political opponents, but completely innocent people, amongst them women and children. He often confessed publicly to all vices and sins, except one sin, to have ever denied God. He believed he could make his peace with God by murder, and to ensure his victims' salvation.

91

privileges. They took over the tasks that the central government had always neglected, such as primary schools, hospitals, etc. In the same years, Alexander II submitted the whole system of law court procedure to reforms modelled on the European example. Legal proceedings became open to the public. Decisions by juries took the place of arbitrary judgement. Russian courts became the most progressive in the world. And that in a country which was, in fact, neither free nor democratic!

RUSSIAN
COUNTRYSIDE

Page 93:
Idyllic snowy village
in the Podmoskovy.
In many parts of Russia,
the 20th century has not yet
touched isolated villages.

Pages 94/95:
Untouched countryside
in the Podmoskovy.

Pages 96/97:
'Mother Volga',
Europe's largest and
mightiest river.
The hard life of the men
who used to pull the boats
upstream and whose
melancholic songs are known
throughout the world,
fed social rebellion.

Pages 98/99:
Bison still live in the
famous wild-life reserve
in White Russia,
the only ones in Europe.

Light and Shadow in the Russian Nature

For centuries the West has had an image of the 'Russian soul' as something boundless, full of fire, full of contradictions. More than by any one characteristic, the Russian is distinguished by the grand contrasts in his nature.

In the *Four Brothers Karamazov,* Dostoevsky portrayed the whole range of the Russian personality. There is the wild, earth-bound sensuality, the stormy, irrational love of Dmitry; Ivan is the intellectual yet deeply religious personality (what western atheist would hold conversations with the devil?); Alyosha is the embodiment of deep piety and the feeling for the community of man, while Smerdyakov expresses the personality of the *kholopstvo,* the cringing servant of a servile community who has lost his consciousness of human dignity.

There you have the Russian! But at the same time Dostoevsky invited the world to appreciate Russia for her greatness and her noble features, and not to condemn her for her infamous acts.

When there are festivities in Russia, the Russians' generosity finds expression, a generosity which, with the consumption of vodka and *sakussi* (the food served with it), and the mounting good spirits, becomes immoderate. One tips back a little glass (in one swallow, of course), a second one, and a third: 'God loves the Holy Trinity'. One talks and talks, and drinks and drinks, and at the same time two or three of the guests have come to blows. There can be no question of calculation or prudence when a festive occasion is in preparation. (Dostoevsky, for example, spent the whole of the money he received for his first book on inviting all his friends, acquaintances, and their friends' friends to a sumptuous feast.) It is part of the tradition of such occasions that all the men should be under the table at the end of the banquet. In the same way it is understood that after the Saint's day of his village, a day spent every year in eating and drinking from noon until midnight, a Russian will spend the following day sleeping off his hangover. This failure to turn up for work, and that because of such a backward, bourgeois institution as a Saint's day, was still officially criticized in 1965. What, it was asked, had happened to the educational work of the local party secretary?

Such universal customs for festive occasions probably also gave officialdom the welcome opportunity for the prohibition of the sale of candles at Christmas. The supposed reason for this is to prevent the 'frequent outbreaks of fire' due no doubt to the combination of vodka and open flames. In reality this prohibition is just another obstacle put in the way of the pious. It is the same with the prohibition against ringing church bells, said to be in the interest of noise abatement.

Russia lives on, though simpler, poorer, in its feasts—and also in its mourning.

For in grief the people know as little restraint as in gaiety. Their sorrow erupts without reserve. Today, in the villages, the wailing women still go to the house of mourning, their whole demeanour expressing unbearable sorrow, tearing their hair and singing for their dead neighbour the beautiful poetic folk dirges. In the Requiem service the dead are mourned with a song of farewell. The priest and the choir accompany the soul with sung prayers while the bells are silent.

The people have put their whole nature into the songs, into the indescribably sorrowful laments as well as into the fiery, gay dance songs of the celebrations.

A concertina leads the songs, the young people accompany it with rhythmical clapping and stamping, then they take each other by the hand and turn in a circle. The song and dance gets faster and faster, first left, then right, the music increases its tempo, then the ring breaks up into pairs. *Kamarinskaya* is such a song, other well-loved, gay folksongs are *Kalinka,* and the boisterous song *Vo ku-, Vo Kuznitse* (In the Forge).

In the Ukraine, in the old days, dance songs were accompanied by the *volunka,* the barrel organ, and today they are still accompanied by the *surna,* especially in Armenia. The Ukrainian song *The Grey Owl's Lament,* or the moving *Sulikon* from Gruzinskaya are sung to the most moving, melancholy melodies. The lover from Gruzinskaya sings with longing of Suliko whom he loved so much and who does not care for him, so that he has to mourn to the end of his life, alone. Just as with the Russian beauty who has lost her ring and, with it, the love of her fiancé, she can find no rest day or night. *Dubinushka* too, and the Stenka Razin song *By the Volga Yawns an Abyss* express in their melancholy the ancient depths of Russian sorrow.

The wealth of Russian music rests strongly on a foundation of poetry and folksong. Thus Pushkin inspired Glinka to write the first Russian opera *Russlan and Ludmilla,* and Tchaikovsky his masterpieces *Eugen Onegin* and *The Queen of Spades.* Anton Rubinstein was stimulated by Lermontov's verse tale to write his opera *Demon.* Rimsky-Korsakov wrote his opera *Christmas Eve* and *May Night* after subjects by Gogol. And Borodin's opera *Prince Igor* is an interpretation of the *Song of Igor.* Many outstanding Russian composers have drawn their ideas and subjects from the works of Nekrassov, Gogol, Tolstoy and Dostoevsky. The work of the best composers of this century, Prokofiev and Stravinsky, also has its roots deep in the fruitful earth of Russian folklore.

The standard of Russian musical interpretation is very high. The whole world applauds the pianists Svatoslav Richter and Emil Gilels, the violinist David Oistrakh, the cellist Rostropovitch, the harpist Olga Erdeli. Everyone knows the Russian song and dance ensembles, the Alexandrov choir of the Army, the Pyatnitsky choir, the choir directed by Sveshnikov, the choirs from Omsk and Voronesh. Not only the music-theatres of Moscow, but those of the provinces also have impressive groups of actors, and the opera ensembles of Leningrad, Kiev, Novosibirsk and Sverdlovsk are given an enthusiastic reception in Moscow.

Wherein lies the strength of our opera houses, what is the secret of their world-wide success? There is only one answer: it lies in the great music of the Russian composers, Glinka, Tchaikovsky, Rimsky-Korsakov, Mussorgsky, Borodin, Rachmaninov, Stravinsky, and the admirable composers who come from the national republics, Lysenko, Paliashvili, Gadchibekov and Komitas. Soviet composers have

Page 103:
The unique city of Odessa. By walking down these steps one can reach the spot alongside which, in 1905, the mutinous battleship 'Potemkin' tied up. Through the film of the same name which was made in 1925 by the great director Sergey Eisenstein, the 'Potemkin' episode became a symbol all over the world.

Page 104:
Dream paradise of every Soviet citizen: the beach at Sochi on the Caucasian bank of the Black Sea.

Page 105:
Holiday visitors in the park of a sanatorium for miners at Sochi at an early session of physical training with military discipline.

composed more than six hundred operas and ballets, yet none of these works has found a place in the permanent programme of the Bolshoi or any first-class theatre. Today Russia's opera suffers the same tragedy as the theatre: the narrow standards of social realism prevent the creation of true works of art. Half a century of Soviet rule has produced only two or three pieces which have had deserved success.

The Russian people love that music which is recognized as timelessly 'Russian', and is a true expression of the Russian nature.

Not only the limitless generosity of the Russian people, but their endless patience is proverbial. This patience can sometimes result in complete inactivity, in spiritual and physical inertia. In Russia this species of patience is called *oblomovshtchina* after the hero of Goncharov's novel *Oblomov,* who, on his divan, gave himself up to unconditional passivity. The obverse side of this patience manifests itself in the endless endurance of inhuman conditions. In how many wars has the Russian soldier made up for the imperfection of his equipment by his courage and tenacity? The energy of the Russian soldier constitutes an enormous potential, and great things could be achieved as long as this energy was properly directed. This was amply demonstrated in the Second World War. The attack on the Soviet Union by the German army on 22nd June 1941 came as a great shock to the inhabitants of the frontier districts and to the Russian troops stationed there. In the first hours after the attack many ran straight into the arms of the alleged 'liberators'. But in the shortest possible time the Government succeeded, as at the time of Napoleon, in mobilizing the whole population against the invaders in a great patriotic war. Soldiers and partisans, the whole Russian people rose with their typical heroic capacity for suffering and with tremendous strength, a strength fed not only by material but by spiritual and moral sources, to defend their country which was threatened by deadly danger, allowing no early setbacks to discourage them.

But when the Russian loses patience, when he revolts, he also knows no limits, reason cannot make itself heard. Pushkin called the Russian insurrection 'senseless and merciless'. He gives an example in his novel *Dubrovsky* in the person of the smith Arkhip who, though himself totally uninvolved, allows the hated representatives of the law, the 'devil's brood' to be burned in the inn, having himself bolted all windows and doors and set fire to the building. But when a little cat pitiably mews on the smouldering roof of a barn, this same Arkhip decides immediately to rescue the little creature, risking his own life, for one must not allow one of God's creatures to perish....

The Russian bear is an excellent symbol of his good nature and latent cruelty. Even more eloquent is the legend of Ilya Muromez, the noble warrior. All of thirty years he sat behind the stove and wouldn't move, however much his brave brothers laughed at him. But when his time came, Ilya shook off his inaction and achieved the greatest deeds of daring to the honour of God and his Prince.

Page 106: The largest waterway of the South is the Dniepr which connects the Black Sea with the canal system of Central Russia and the Baltic. Among such people, where friendly, uncalculating cordiality alternates with dark, incalculable pursuits of dark aims and forces, one is never safe from surprises. But one does not meet such authentic Russians so often nowadays. For too long officialdom has praised only the Smerdyakov in the Russian character. But amongst the youth of today, Alyosha is again amongst the people, and his spirit will surely determine the character of the Russia of the future.

Faith, Foundation of Russian Culture

The deep piety of our people, possibly thought naïve by intellectual Westerners, has set its seal on the whole spiritual life of Russia. It also partly determined Russia's relationship with the West, and its foreign politics which have been based on the attitude of the people as a whole. It was Orthodoxy which determined Russia's relationship with Byzantium. When Eastern Rome had become the stronghold of the infidels, Russia's undeviating aim was to set up the Cross once more over the Crescent. The unmistakable symbol created to express these messianic aspirations, this confidence in the victory of Christian Russia, was the Cross above a recumbent Crescent open at the top. Within her own order, which was accepted and even loved as God-willed, Christian humility reigned. In our own time, the regime has tried to placate the Russian people with a substitute religion. It does not lack a characteristic messianism: the claim to 'redeem' the world. And the Soviet proletariat is supposed to put itself at the disposal of, to sacrifice itself to this ideal! But where is the confidence in the victory of this pseudo-dogma of salvation? And where has the people's joy in sacrifice gone? What has survived of it turns again towards the truth. My people are finding their way back, faith is once again entering their lives.

Even in the face of a confrontation between rationalism and realism, Russia remains indebted to faith. For what kind of an atheist is Ivan Karamazov? Does his reason answer his questions about God? He wouldn't be talking with the devil then! Though an atheist, he remains religious. This is also true of the 'God-deniers', one of whom we meet in Dostoevsky's *Brothers Karamazov*. This poor cripple wants to avenge himself. He wants to *kill* Christ. He goes to church, takes Communion, he keeps the body and blood of the living Christ in his mouth, hoarding the most sublime life. Once outside, he wraps the Host in a small cloth and fires at it, he *shoots* Christ. Where but in Russia would one find such passion, and such belief even in the refusal to believe?

This inescapable relationship with religion and supernatural matters is reflected in Russian literature. The realist Gogol, for example, in *The Nose, The Image, The Nevski Prospect,* moves always on the frontiers of delirium. And it is no different in his book, *The Overcoat,* from which, according to Dostoevsky, all later literature stems. Finally Dostoevsky himself is a comprehensive realist, that is one who does not only see material reality, but also irrational, spiritual reality. As such he used, long before the *avant-garde* of the West, the stream-of-consciousness method as the only way of expressing this reality, both for Raskolnikov and in the *Brothers Karamazov*.

THE BALTIC
PROVINCES

The Baltic Provinces, today's Soviet Republics of Lithuania, Latvia and Estonia, were, in the Middle Ages, conquered by the Teutonic Knights. In the course of the 17th and 18th centuries, Sweden, in accordance with her Baltic policy, extended her control over the whole of the Baltic States including that district around the mouth of the Neva where Leningrad stands today. After the Battle of Poltava (1709), Peter the Great annexed the whole of the Baltic region. After twenty years of independence (1920–40), the Baltic States became once again part of Russia.

*Page 109:
The Dvina flows through Latvia; its course, mostly between wooded banks, is very picturesque.*

III

Pages 110/111:
View from the right bank,
of the Dvina towards Riga
the capital of Latvia.
Riga was founded in 1201
by the Canon of
Bremen Cathedral,
Albert von Appeldern.
He conquered Latvia
at the head of a 'crusade'.
The architecture is German
in character;
Riga did considerable trade
with the Hanseatic towns.

Pages 112/113:
Right: Riga's German
architectural character
is not only evident in
the shape of the towers
of the town and her churches,
but also in secular buildings
where Gothic and
Renaissance elements
mix strangely.
The house in this picture
was the most beautiful in
Riga. Unfortunately it
was destroyed in one
of the battles of the
Second World War.
Left: Fortifications
at Tallinn,
the former Reval,
and the Church of
St. Olaf.

Pages 114/115:
View of the old town
of Tallinn,
the capital of Estonia.
From afar one sees first,
standing on a small hill
in the centre of the town,
its landmark, the cathedral
built in traditional
Russian style.

Page 116:
Winter solitude
in a small Lithuanian
village.

In the same way the literary epoch of Romanticism was also dominated by religion. An exalted beauty from some old distinguished family would often take the veil and give herself completely to her heavenly bridegroom—both in literature and in real life. In boarding-schools the daughters of noble families were brought up in the spirit of good breeding and Orthodoxy, and in total ignorance of the things of this world. This picture of the Russian girl was immortalized by Shukovsky, master of Russian romanticism, in his ballad *Svetlana*.

Of the young men, Lensky (from Pushkin's *Eugen Onegin*) might be taken as the ideal of romanticism. Love, roses, and nightingales are the symbols of his tenderness, he writes poems in the album of his adored. He wears his hair curled (like the young Pushkin himself), 'and he who despises all of life's colourful glory, would soon be eighteen'.

During the second half of the 19th century, Russian romanticism blossomed into a phenomenon described, for example, by Turgenyev in *Virgin Soil*. Young people, students, 'went amongst the people'. As a kind of voluntary practitioners they went to the many villages where there was neither school nor doctor, they taught, helped the sick, and preached their ideas about human dignity. Basarov, the progressive-idealistic student in Turgenyev's novel *Fathers and Children* explained the necessary steps the Government should take to achieve an 'enlightenment' of the people. And indeed it was the achievement of the local administration of the *semstvo* that before 1917 almost 80 per cent of the population had at least some elementary education. A fifth of the population was illiterate.

The neo-romantic movement which, at the turn of the century, was represented above all by the leading figure of Vladimir Solovyov, but also by Alexander Blok and Andrey Bely, had definite religious and mystical characteristics. At this time many new sects arose, the *bogoiskatelstvo* (God-seekers) became fashionable, and 'prophets' grew in the fruitful soil of Russian piety like mushrooms after the rain.

Russia's characteristic romanticism lives on in the works of Pasternak, Olga Bergholz, Marina Zvetayeva, Mandelstam and Gumilev.

I welcome the movement known as SMOG (the initials of the Russian words for courage, youth, form and depth) as a true romantic renaissance. The young members of this literary and artistic organization have, in our decade, declared war against the philistines and Tchekists, against mediocrity and ignorance, and have begun to give emphasis again to the soul.

The Russian people approached philosophical thought rather late in their development. It is significant that at the beginning of the 19th century, the dramatist Alexander Segeyvitch Griboyedov expressed in the title of his comedy *Intellect Causes Suffering* what was felt by the society of the day. Until the end of the 18th century Christian belief and Orthodoxy filled the Russian people with such uninterrupted intensity that they felt no need for the philosophical interpretation of life. Also, unlike the Europeans of the Middle Ages, they did not suffer from the fear that the world of reason and the world of faith might suddenly fall apart. It was this fear that drove the great Thomas Aquinas (1225 to 1274) to try to prove in his *Summa Theologica* that reason and faith are only apparently contradictory, and this only because reason is too limited to encompass the enigma of faith. The faith of the Russian people was indistinguishable from their very existence, and therefore they were not at all tempted to

117

examine the substance of that faith to see whether it would stand up before the tribunal of reason. It is therefore significant that so important a Russian thinker as Sergey Bulgakov, in his work *The Tragedy of Philosophy,* compared the history of philosophy to the human tragedy: like Icarus, the human philosopher tried to approach the sun, complete knowledge, but it was impossible for him to avoid plunging to the earth. For philosophy wants to create the world from its own principles, and must experience the tragic lesson that thinking and being are not identical.

But for the religious consciousness thinking and being are identical, one cannot be detached from the other. It is therefore not to be wondered at that this basic phenomenon influenced Russian philosophy. Taking into account the religious tradition, it was almost a matter of necessity that Russian philosophy should take on an existentialist character. Unlike the West European, the Russian does not philosophize about thought and logic, and he formulates no theories of perception. He broods over the problems of existence and self-realization, about the nature of human freedom, its metaphysical limits and its realization in individual, social and historical life. No nation in the world has thought about freedom so comprehensively and with such metaphysical insight as the Russian. In the name of the freedom of the personality, the Russian nihilists declared war on idealism and belief. Those philosophers who were led to philosophy from the truths of evangelical thought were even more passionate in their search for the spiritual foundation and existential deepening of freedom. From a long line of such men I shall name only three here: Dostoevsky (as a poet, a passionate philosopher of freedom), Vladimir Solovyov and Nikolay Berdayev whose extensive work *The Philosophy of the Free Spirit* is one of the undisputed standard works of our century on the philosophy of freedom. The most Russian of all Russian philosophers is Nikolay Fedorovitch Fedorov (1828 to 1903) who is little known in western Europe. His fundamental theme is contained in his chief work *Philosophy of Common Action.*

The Holy-Trinity Monastery of St. Sergius at Sagorsk, which is still inhabited by monks and holds the only seminary in the Soviet Union, is an ancient place of pilgrimage of the Russian people. The Monastery was founded in 1340 when St. Sergius built a small wooden church on this hill. The time of Ivan the Terrible was the Monastery's golden age. At that time it owned about a hundred and twenty thousand serfs. Around the original sanctuary a great many buildings have been added. In the middle rises a high, four-storey clock

This represents Russia's answer to questions raised by German idealism on the one hand and Karl Marx on the other. Fedorov believes fervently that it is man's task to realize God's dominion on earth. According to his interpretation, the Christian Last Judgement represents a threat from God. To escape this judgement, men must unite in 'common action'. With the help of science and technology they must fight against the elementary, irrational and deadly forces of nature. He believed that by activating all his powers, man would become capable of organizing cosmic life, of conquering death itself, and of raising the dead to new life, so that he could step immediately from this life into the eternal life promised by Christ. Almost in the same words as Marx and Engels, Fedorov demands of philosophy that it should not only recognize the world, but that it should change it, freeing life from evil and sorrow, but chiefly from death as the source of all evil. Fedorov's philosophy differed from Communism in its Christian belief. But he agreed with Communism in its demand for action, in his belief in the enormous power of technology, his enmity to capitalism, his denial of purely theoretical thinking, and in his recognition of work as the most necessary basis of human life. When Berdayev calls Fedorov a Communist with a religious foundation, this is theoretically true. But Soviet Russian Communism gives the lie to Fedorov's model philosophy, since the 'common action' does not have the essential religious basis which gives it its meaning. Fedorov's concept that man,

118

under the sign of freedom, could conquer the earth, death and the cosmos, and, victorious, enter straight into eternal life, is nevertheless very 'Russian'.

The truth is that the various currents of philosophy in Russia have always grown out of the foundations of faith, and even when they have gone against belief have been inextricably bound up with it. The same is true of the pictorial and plastic arts which, from the beginning, served and adorned religious life. Brought from Byzantium at the same time as Christianity, both the painting of icons and church architecture became a part of Russian life. It is strange to see the conservative character of this art taken over from Byzantium, and how, through the centuries, the forms have retained the same, unchanging formula which only some distinguished masters have varied from time to time.

It is unlikely that religious painting has so prominent and almost exclusive a place in the national art of any other country.

Let us look at some examples. The best place to do so is in the Moscow Kremlin.

In front of me lies Sobornya Square, once the lively centre of the Kremlin. Today it is empty of life. The large square is surrounded by buildings of white stone, motionless and silent. All the Kremlin is white and gold.

tower. It was built by Rastrelli in the years 1741 to 1767. To its right one can see the domes of the Cathedral of the Assumption, on the left side of the picture the Church of the Holy Trinity, where there is the grave of St. Sergius. The whole group of buildings is surrounded by a huge wall as fortification, and which made it possible for the monastery to withstand the onslaught of thirty thousand Poles at the 'time of the troubles' (1608 to 1618). (Engraving after a painting from the turn of the century.)

The ancient Cathedral of the Assumption was built in 1475 by the famous Italian architect Rodolfo Fioravanti in the Lombard-Byzantine style after the model of the 12th-century Dimitry church in Vladimir. The cathedral is crowned by a dome about one hundred and fifty feet high, and four smaller cupolas. Above its door there is a beautiful fresco of the Madonna and Child painted by Semyon Ushakov. The impression of lightness which one gets from this bright painting and the radiant white and gold of the cathedral is quickly changed when one goes inside. The walls are covered with frescoes showing scenes of the Last Judgement. The vaulted ceiling is painted with episodes from the life of Christ, the Madonna and various Saints.

The Russian Tsars were crowned in the Cathedral of the Assumption. Along the walls are the graves of the most important Metropolitans of Moscow. This house of God seems to symbolize the fate of Russia: more than once the cathedral was stormed by enemies, set on fire, robbed, but each time it was built up again in a short time, and each time it became more beautiful.

The iconostasis of the Cathedral of the Assumption is a collection of masterpieces, a veritable treasure-chest of Russian iconography. Its greatest treasure is the 12th-century icon of the Madonna of Vladimir which was brought to Moscow in 1395 by Prince Dimitry Donskoy to protect the city from the Tartars. On its right there is an icon of the Redeemer which was painted by the Byzantine emperor Manuilos.

Here in the Cathedral of the Assumption I always have a particularly strong feeling of the origins of Russian life, of the people who called their country 'Holy Russia'. And I feel there most strongly that only in God, in the lap of the Orthodox Church, is there an organic life for our people. One of my French friends once admitted to me: 'The Kremlin reminds me more of a monastery than of a palace or a citadel.'

In the neighbouring *Ris Polosheny* church, there are the wonderful frescoes and icons by the Master Nasar Istomin. (Ris Polosheny is the name for the decorated metal covering of icons which leaves only the face and hands of the figure free.) The church was built in 1484 by a group of architects from Pskov.

The Cathedral of the Annunciation too, the most magnificent and yet the most tender of Moscow's churches, was the work of Pskov architects. Its gilded roof with ten domes, a gallery, the stone portals ornamented in early renaissance style, and the wonderful mosaic floors of ancient precious stones delight the visitor. The strange frescoes on the walls and roof represent prophets, patriarchs and philosophers of classical Greece, there are scenes from the Gospels, illustrations of the Apocalypse, and episodes from the life of the Byzantine emperors. There is a beautiful iconostasis. Its icons were painted at the beginning of the 15th century by the famous Masters Andrey Rublev, Theophanes Grek and Prokhor Gorodets.

The Cathedral of the Archangel is the 'foreigner' among the Kremlin churches. It was built in 1509 by the Milan architect Novi in the place of an older church of the Archangel Michael, and it is a good example of Milan architecture of the late Renaissance. In this church lie the sarcophagi with the mortal remains of forty-seven Moscow Princes and the grave of Peter II. Beautiful frescoes cover the walls, works by the Masters Theophanus Grek and Semyon Tchorny. Especially impressive are the frescoes of the 'Foreign Ambassadors being introduced to Prince Vladimir' and 'The Baptism of Vladimir of Russia'. Their colours have not faded more in the course of time than has the glory of Kiev Russia which began the tradition of the painting of icons.

The first icons in Kiev, Novgorod, Vladimir and Suzdal were painted by Theophanes Grek who came to Novgorod from Constantinople in the 14th century. Under his direction, his pupils and successors founded a school of icon painting which eventually became known as the Yaroslav school. Quite early on, Theophanes devoted himself exclusively to the work in the Kremlin churches. Two monks from the monastery of the Holy Trinity at Sagorsk came to help him: the icon painter Prokhor Gorodets and his pupil Andrey Rublev.

Rublev was without doubt the greatest icon painter of his time. Little is known of his life. Even his date of birth (about 1360) cannot be definitely fixed. The only thing that is certain is that he entered the monastery of Sagorsk while still young, and that he worked as the apprentice of the icon painter Prokhor. In 1404 he went to Svenigorod. Three icons from that time have been preserved, one of the Redeemer, one of the Archangel Michael, and one of the Apostle Paul, and these are now in the Tretyakov Gallery. Though some parts have faded, the icons are astonishing in their harmony of colour, their humanity, and their strong linear quality. Later Rublev entered the Androyevsky monastery and there painted the walls of the monastery church. A few years later he travelled to Vladimir where he painted the frescoes of the Church of the Assumption. Then he returned to Moscow. Andrey Rublev ended his life in the monastery of the Holy Trinity at Sagorsk. He died around the year 1427. His best-known works are the icon of the Holy Trinity, of the Assumption and that of St. John.

In the second half of the 15th century another icon painter came to prominence— Dionissy. He differs from the severely realistic manner of Theophanes Grek and Rublev by using a more impressionist style.

At the end of the 15th and the beginning of the 16th century Moscow experienced a golden age. At this time the wealthy nobility built chapels in their houses and on their estates, and the icon painters were overwhelmed with work. It was now that the

This pencil sketch by the Russian painter Ryepin shows Count Leo Tolstoy at his writing-table. Neither Pushkin nor Dostoevsky had, during their lifetime, such an effect on the whole world as did Tolstoy. His nature was full of strange contradictions. He postulated the ideal of complete chastity and wrote the artistically perfect novel of the break-up of a marriage, Anna Karenina. He acknowledged himself to be an uncompromising

school of Stroganov gained its importance, founded by the family of Stroganov in Perm. Later all the masters of this school moved to Moscow. The school of Stroganov took its basic principles from the school of Novgorod, but, once in Moscow, became very much influenced by the West. The ascetic severity of the figures gives way to strength of expression and a realistic liveliness in the execution of the face. At the time of Peter the Great the West European style began to predominate, but at the same time the highly developed art of the icon painter started to decline until it was no more than a formal craft. After the Revolution most of the schools of painting were closed, some changed their emphasis like the school of Palekh. Its painted lacquer boxes are world-famous and compare with Persian miniatures in the perfection of their smallest details.

In the Russia of today, nobody paints icons. Innumerable ancient masterpieces are not a part of church services any more, but frequently hang (if they have not vanished abroad) in the churches which have been turned into museums.

The Italian Rastrelli, who came to Russia at the beginning of the 18th century with his father, who was a sculptor, brought the West European style to the country of the Tsars, but with his wonderful gift of sympathetic understanding he was able to adapt it to express the Russian nature. As court architect to Elizabeth (from 1741) he had plenty of opportunity to do so, especially in Petersburg where his talent had the greatest scope.

The centre of Petersburg's religious life today is the Nikolsky Cathedral, the largest church in Russia, where religious services are still held. It holds more than six thousand people and was built in 1762 by Tchevakinsky. He was obviously influenced by Rastrelli since his work bears some resemblance to the Smolny Cathedral in the same city, a great work of Rastrelli's. In every architectural detail one feels his desire to add yet more decoration to the church, to give it a splendid, rich and noble appearance. The white marble columns in front of the blue façade are particularly beautiful, the window frames decorated with the heads of cherubs, and the oval upper windows surrounded by stucco garlands. Next to the church stands the clock tower with decorative columns and, inside, a beautiful iconostasis carved of wood. The slender tower is reflected in the waters of the canal.

All the other great cathedrals of Petersburg were made into museums after the Revolution, but they seem only to be waiting to hear the Word of God pronounced once more. For despite all repressions by the State, the number of the faithful and their religious consciousness grows steadily. Especially on holy days, churches everywhere which are still allowed to function, are full to overflowing. More and more young people attend the services. And the faithful once more go on pilgrimages to the monastery of the Holy Trinity at Sagorsk, to make obeisance before the miraculous Icon.

The icon has also found a place in Orthodox homes once again, an eternal light, a little oil lamp, often stands beside it. One of my good friends who, being 'suspect', was not infrequently visited by a member of the secret police, used to seat his uninvited guests opposite a large icon. And when one of them once pointed to it and remarked patronizingly: 'How can you allow such tasteless stuff around? We've got beyond that sort of thing. Science has long ago proved that man's ancestors....' My friend interrupted: '*You* are descended from the apes. *I* was created by God!'

The *Russians* were created by God.

The Russian Country

In my imagination I survey the whole limitless expanse of my native country. And as in a wonderful dream, I see the road our country has taken, starting from our capital city. It strove at all times towards the sunrise, just as Prince Vladimir, 'the beautiful sun', had led it. It is as if Kiev, and later Muscovite Russia, had been a magnet which attracted to itself countries both near and far. And thus, step by step, century after century, the present-day Russia emerged, and under the sign of the Russian nation, a family of peoples was born.

In the west, Galicia and Carpatho-Russia, Bukovinia and Bessarabia, White Russia and Lithuania, Volhinia and Posolia, Latvia and Estonia and Karelia were united with the original Russia. In the east, the principalities of Ryazan and Vladimir-Suzdal joined, the Khanates of Kazan and Astrakhan, and the whole Tartar Golden Horde. The Russian explorers set out and found the way to the Taiga and the Tundra, the Arctic Ocean and to Siberia. In the Urals and Trans-Urals iron-ore, all kinds of metals, and every kind of precious stone were found. Yermak brought Russia an incredible present, the whole immense Siberia. Its forests are priceless, green gold, under its earth lie vast quantities of uranium, iron and coal, oil and rare metals, gold and diamonds. The explorers Khabarov and Nevelsky discovered the fabulous country beside the Amur and the vast spaces of the Far East. Russia pushed forward as far as the Pacific Ocean and even beyond it, to the Sakhalin and Kuril Islands.

Nor did the warriors of the south sleep. They conquered the Bashkir steppes and the steppes of Nogay with their immense flocks of sheep, cattle and wild horses, the wide open spaces of Novorossysks and the Black Sea, the Crimea and the Caucasus, Daghestan, Gruzinskaya, Armenia, Azerbaijan, Uzbekistan and Tajikstan, Kazakhstan and Kirghiz. And there it lies before us, the great Russian country. From the Arctic Ocean to the southern seas, from the Baltic to the Pacific its open spaces stretch, its mountains rise, its valleys are green, mighty rivers flow and waterfalls plunge down, the jets of the geysers shoot into the air, its songs, its glory....

A sixth of the earth....

More than twelve million square miles.

Let us look closely at a few square miles. The Caucasus for example. It would be difficult to find any other part of the world with which to compare it. It is a country all by itself, reaching from the Black Sea to the Caspian. Across it the migration of the nations passed and each nation left traces of its passing. Today about two hundred different kinds of people still live in the Caucasus, some inhabiting but three villages, each with its own language which nobody else understands.

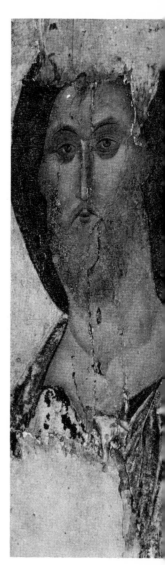

Icon of the Redeemer by Andrey Rublev in the Tretyakov Gallery in Moscow (Detail). The artistic importance of Rublev to religious painting is comparable to that of Fra Angelico.

The key to the Caucasus is Rostov on the Don, a large, gay southern town with a very mixed population. Once many Greeks lived here, and today there are probably more Armenians than Russians in the town. Nearby lies Novotcherkask, formerly the residence of the Ataman of the Don Cossack army. Both towns have lived through a great deal. In Rostov the staff of the Voluntary (White) Army was stationed with Denikin, Wrangel and Shuko. The Kornilov campaign started from here and the Cossacks Bogayevsky, Kaledin and Krasnov gave bloody battle to the Bolsheviks. Twice, in 1918 and 1942, the Germans were here.

The district of Krasnodar is beautiful. It is the granary of southern Russia with its famous Kuban wheat. What wonderful bread the Cossack women baked from it on cabbage leaves! Food for the gods. One doesn't find such bread any more today. And the fruit and vegetable gardens, the melon fields of the Kuban! But the greatest treasure of the Kuban district is the belt of health resorts which reaches from the isthmus of Kerch to Gruzinskaya. The whole district of the Black Sea, from Rumania to Turkey, is a recreation area.

How splendid is Taman, once the country of Tmutarakan. Today it is a dead city. It is true that there are excavations in progress, but they are going very slowly. The endless reed banks of the Kuban with their many birds stretch on and on. One can even see flamingoes there. The enormous reed forests produce the excellent pressed reed sheets used for building cottages, stables and barns. And I am thinking of course most of all of the Taman of Lermontov, of Petchorin* and the tragic fate of his author. The resorts of Mineralny Vody are forever connected with Lermontov's name. Here Princess Mary* suffered, in another place the poet himself. And there he was killed, at the foot of the Mashuk. Many Russian writers were inspired by the Caucasus: Pushkin, Lermontov, Griboyedov, Bestruchev-Marlinsky, Tolstoy.

Probably most characteristic of the life of the Caucasian mountain people is Daghestan, its mountains, valleys, rushing rivers and high mountain lakes. Some of its rivers have been tamed: the power-stations of Gergebilsk and Sulak provide the whole of Daghestan with electricity. The capital of the Republic, Makhachkala, is an important harbour on the Caspian Sea. The second big harbour is Derbent, an ancient town which played a part even in Sassanian times. Its small white houses, the clay garden enclosures, the little donkeys on the narrow mountain tracks, remind one of times long ago. The leaves on the olive trees rustle gently. Grapes ripen in Derbent where Alexander the Great halted on his way to India. More than a million people live in Daghestan but it is far from being a unit as a country. People speak different languages which no European understands. The largest group of people are the Avars; they form a quarter of the population. After this come the Lezgians, Kumyks, Dargins, Nogays, Tartars and others. They all have their own customs, their own language and their own way of living. For decades they fought against Russia under their great general Shamil. Only after Shamil had been captured and Hadji Murat, another renowned leader of the mountain people, killed, did the fortunes of war turn to Russia.

The Daghestan mountain people are not only good horticulturists but also excellent craftsmen. Whole towns (Aouls) have specialized in this or that craft. The Daghestan goldsmiths were world-famous. Their gold-mounted, inlaid weapons, and their belts decorated with metal discs were unique. Wood and stone carvers

123

decorated whole towns with their monuments and gravestones. Young and old were busy with knotting carpets. There were towns in which all the old men were busy expounding the Koran; other towns provided the whole world with tight-rope walkers. I once found myself in a town where all the inhabitants were professional beggars. They roamed the country carrying long staffs and collecting alms. Some even became rich.

Again, there is Aoul Tchokh which reminds one of a huge amphitheatre. The houses ascend the mountain on eleven terraces. Each house is dug out of the rock, all have but a single storey. The ground floor has a kitchen and stable, above there is the *Kunatskaya,* the living room, covered with carpets, runners and cushions. Only the stove downstairs is heated and there the old people sleep. In the Kunatskaya it is colder than out of doors. More than once I have slept in a friend's Kunatskaya, but I must confess that only after a glass of vodka could I get warm between the icy sheets and my felt coat.

The people have no easy life. There is little earth, only smooth rock and stony terraces. One meets men, and often women, dragging heavy sacks full of soil from the valley, to heap up layers of earth on the terraces, making a small field or a garden where fruit and vegetables are cultivated. Yes, the mountain people lead a hard life, but they will not leave their mountains for anything in the world. They love their free life and nature all around them. Tanned by wind and sun, they are known for their wonderful health and the great age they reach. I have known mountain people who were over a hundred years old and still hale and hearty.

The most beautiful of the holiday resorts is Sochi, founded in 1911. It is like a great garden, its houses almost invisible. Not only the innumerable parks and famous tree nurseries, each courtyard, every sanatorium, the pavements and the streets vanish amongst the foliage of palms, magnolias, oleander, eucalyptus trees and Japanese cedars, acacia, weeping willows, cypresses and poplars. The public gardens are full of huge dark red zinnias, antirrhinums, azaleas and purple chrysanthemums, and their symphony of colours makes a wonderful sight against the background of tree-covered mountains and the blue of the sea. Sochi, honoured by many ministers as their holiday resort, has been hardly within reach of the ordinary citizen. Only recently a series of large hotels have been built there to supplement the original one.

One of the most spectacular corners of Gruzinskaya is Cape Pitsunda, covered with three-thousand-year-old mammoth trees. In ancient times one of the most important cities of the world stood here. A Byzantine church of the 5th century remains. Today it still has its original plaster in the interior without a single crack. Here a wonderful beneficent silence reigns, and it seems as if the huge trees stand on sentry duty protectively near the water. The sea is always mirror-smooth, there are no gales in the natural harbour. In recent years a huge holiday resort has been built here.

In Gagra, too, one can have a wonderful rest. The green cape with its unique botanical gardens is a great centre of attraction.

Adjoining Daghestan lies Chechen-Ingush. Its capital is Grozny, an industrial city and centre of the petroleum industry but hardly typically Caucasian. In any case I must admit that I see the essential Russia in all the national and autonomous Republics which have become part of the former empire. This is not surprising, since,

124

Page 125:
Gruzinskaya's ancient
capital of Mzcheti
is today a town of museums.
The castle was rebuilt
as a prison;
its most prominent prisoner
was Maxim Gorky.

Pages 126/127:
Huge oil drilling
installations advance
ever further into the
Caspian Sea.

Pages 128/129:
The Caucasian mountain
ridges under their eternal
snow reach approximately
16,000 feet.

Pages 130/131:
Harvest on a huge tea
plantation in Chakvi
near Batumi.
Top-quality tea is picked
by hand.

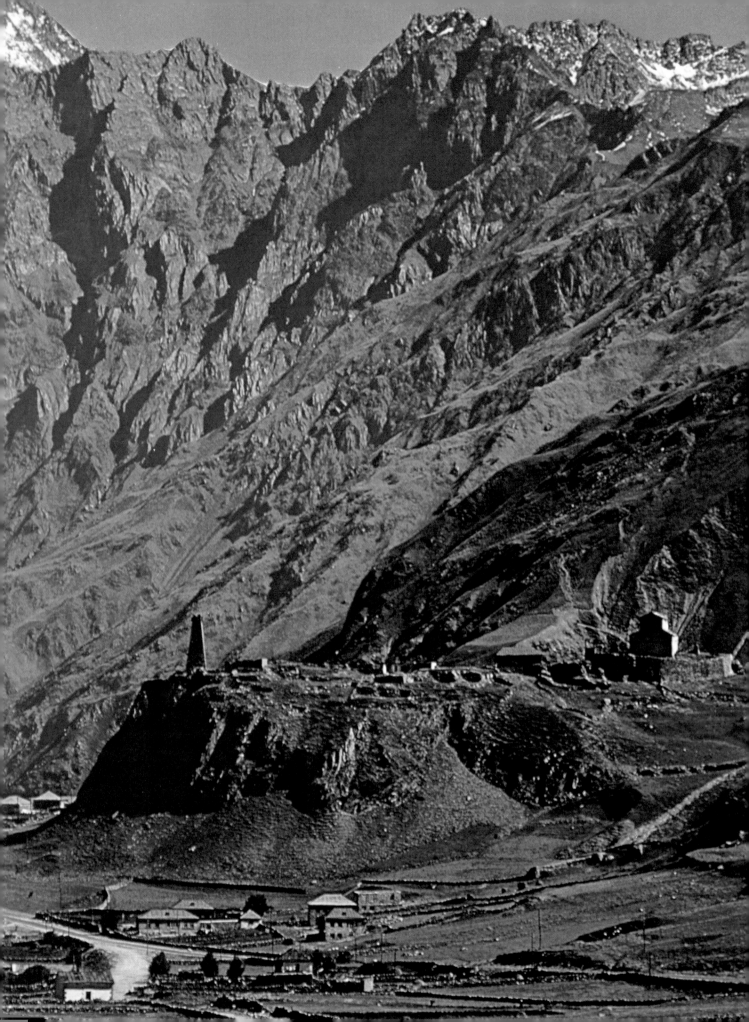

while the old people still speak their former national language, the young people who work in the factories have learnt to speak Russian in the high schools. In all the national Republics there are Russian theatres, schools and libraries. The strongly pronounced nationalism of former times has decreased perceptibly, and all the different nations seem to understand that Russia can only be strong and powerful when there are no national and social disputes.

Central Asia too, her southern steppes are Russia.

Kazakhstan – not so very long ago this name did not even exist. In Europe one hardly knew of the existence of this country, most people imagined it to be part of boundless Siberia. But Kazakhstan is itself a huge country about half the size of Europe. Until the recent past it was almost totally uninhabited. Herds of sheep, horses and cattle roamed the steppes and savannas. The Beys of Kazakh counted their sheep only by the thousands. They lived richly. They ate hardly any bread and every family ate a whole roast sheep for dinner.

Kazakhstan has a comparatively short history. The present-day capital Alma-Ata, meaning 'father of the apple trees' was founded in 1854. Twenty years later it had barely twenty thousand inhabitants. Its colourfully mixed population was composed of Russians, Kazakhs, Chinese and Dungans, and was almost exclusively engaged in agriculture. In the spring practically all the inhabitants went up into the mountains with their sheep to graze them on the Alpine pastures on the mountain range of Zailiisk Alatau. There are still active volcanoes among these mountains; in 1887 and 1910 big earthquakes caused a lot of damage.

Today Kazakhstan's agriculture has received a new impetus, around the town of Zelinograd (from *zelina*, new land) a wide belt of land has in the last decade been put under the plough. But it would have been better to leave the land as pasture for the herds; Kazakhstan's future does not depend on its fields. Its industry, especially in metals, has made great advances. Huge deposits of copper by the Balkash sea form the foundation of a copper smelting works, a steel factory with a planned production of several million tons of steel per year is being built (the building has been going on for the last twelve years).

After Kazakhstan, Uzbekistan is the largest Republic of Central Asia. With its ten million inhabitants it is third, after the Russian and Ukrainian republics.

Uzbekistan's agriculture is typical of a dry, tropical region. Its main crop is cotton. Vegetables are grown in the intensively cultivated gardens. Vegetables and cotton bring in most of the revenue.

Like most central Asian cities, Tashkent, the capital of Uzbekistan, is divided into an Asiatic old city and the new town which is European in character. But Samarkand and Bokhara are much older than the capital. Samarkand in particular presents, with its mosques, mausoleums, minarets and Ulugbek Medresseh, a unique monument of the distant past. And it will for ever remain a monument to the great Tamburlaine, the terrible Mongol who conquered so much of Eastern Europe and the Middle East in the 14th century. The Bibi-Khanum minaret and the ruins of the mosque of the same name are memorials to his favourite wife who is said to have been the extraordinarily beautiful daughter of the Emperor of China.

Turkmenia and Tajikstan are also Russian, though Persian is spoken here.

Page 132:
This 'Aoul', as the towns in the northern Caucasus are called, is named Kubakhi. It lies in the Republic of Daghestan and looks back over more than a thousand years of history. Jewellery, work in gold, swords and daggers decorated with precious stones all come from Kubakhi and are known all over the world.

Page 133:
A monk in front of the entrance to the Geghard Monastery. In the Middle Ages this was the most famous spiritual and cultural centre of Armenia. Its wildly romantic position in the valley of Azat, and its ingenuous architecture attract many tourists today.

Page 134:
The Armenian plateau near the Turkish border. In the background is Mount Ararat on which, according to the Bible, Noah landed his Ark.

Page 135:
Gruzinian girl.

Page 136:
Gruzinian military road which climbs the Caucasus and is still of military importance today. On the rock ledge in the middle of the picture stands the castle of the Tamara, the legend of which Lermontov used in his poem Demon, *and Anton Rubinstein in his opera.*

137

Kirghizia, the youngest of the Central Asian Republics, has recently experienced a stormy period. Its economy depends on the cattle raised in the mountains. And elegant women everywhere want caracul from Kirghizia. It is also famous for its wonderful mountain lake Issyk Kul with its subterranean mineral springs which led to the construction of many sanatoria.

Russia also comprises Armenia, an equally ancient country whose lot has been as hard as that of its neighbours Gruzinskaya and Azerbaijan. In actual fact these countries were never centralized, independent states, but were an easy prey for countless conquerors. Mongols, Persians, Turks terrorized and plundered these small neighbours. In the 18th century a new mediator of the Caucasus appeared upon the scene: Russia. It did not take her long to take all of Armenia from the Persians. During the 19th century, Armenia fought for her independence and lost half of her population.

Today Armenia is torn in two parts, one part belongs to the Soviet Union, the other to Turkey. But only a small section of the Armenian people live there. In Moscow alone there are twice as many Armenians as in Erevan and there is hardly a corner of the world without an Armenian minority.

Outwardly Armenia hardly resembles a Soviet State. In Erevan there are beautiful country houses in neo-classic, Greek, neo-Armenian and Mediterranean style. Armenia can afford to build beautiful houses, not standardized living barracks as one sees in Moscow and in other Russian cities.

Azerbaijan is a country of oil. Even Marco Polo, the Venetian world traveller, described the 'unquenchable torches' he saw there. Almost the whole of the south-eastern part of the country is today covered with a forest of drilling-towers, complete islands of steel reaching deep into the Caspian Sea. Baku, the capital of Azerbaijan, the 'black city', is a maze of drilling-towers, industrial installations and petrol refineries. The upper part of the city, on the other hand, is very beautiful, since oil brought it prosperity a long time ago.

Russia has acquired enormous territories, the Caucasus, Central Asia and Siberia, by force, but she has never had the attitude of Western colonialists. Russia did not systematically exterminate all native people and confine the few that remained into reservations, but integrated them quite naturally, *lived with* her new peoples. Russia did not treat the population of the conquered provinces as her property and an inferior race to be used to feather her nest; on the contrary, the conquerors themselves set to work and opened up new territories not only for their own gain but to the advantage of the original inhabitants. The cultural influence was often reciprocal. Non-Russians have made important contributions to Russian culture. Skovoroda, who founded the school of Russian philosophy in the 18th century, was an Ukrainian, Vashap Shavel a noteworthy poet from Gruzinskaya. Pasternak has translated his work and also that of his contemporary compatriot, Tizian Tabidza, into Russian. Yury Yanovsky was, I believe, the most important Russian-Ukrainian writer of our time. And the world-famous painter Saryan, who does not concern himself with socialist realism, is an Armenian.

It has even been possible for a *Georgian* to occupy the seat of absolute power (and of the most terrible crimes). To the end of his days as a tyrant Stalin spoke with a strong Georgian accent.

MOHAMMEDAN RUSSIA

Page 139:
Turkemen Shepherd.
He doesn't take his wool cap
off either summer or winter
since it protects him
equally from heat
and cold.

Pages 140/141:
A herd of sheep wander
through the Kirghiz uplands.
In the background the
mighty Tien-Shan Massif.

Pages 142/143:
Left: Pious Mohammedans
at prayer. A majority
of the Mohammedan
population follow strictly
the rules of the Koran.
It is remarkable that the
pious Mohammedans,
as opposed to the Orthodox
Christians and the Jews,
have been treated well
by the Soviet Regime.
Middle: Return from
market in the Uzbek town
of Bokhara. The white
turban is the sign of a
religious Mohammedan.
Right:
Itinerant photographer
in a Kishlak (Uzbek
name for a village).

Pages 144/145:
Dromedaries looking for
their favourite food,
the hard leaves of the
Saskaoul and camel thorn
in the burning sand desert
of Central Turkestan.

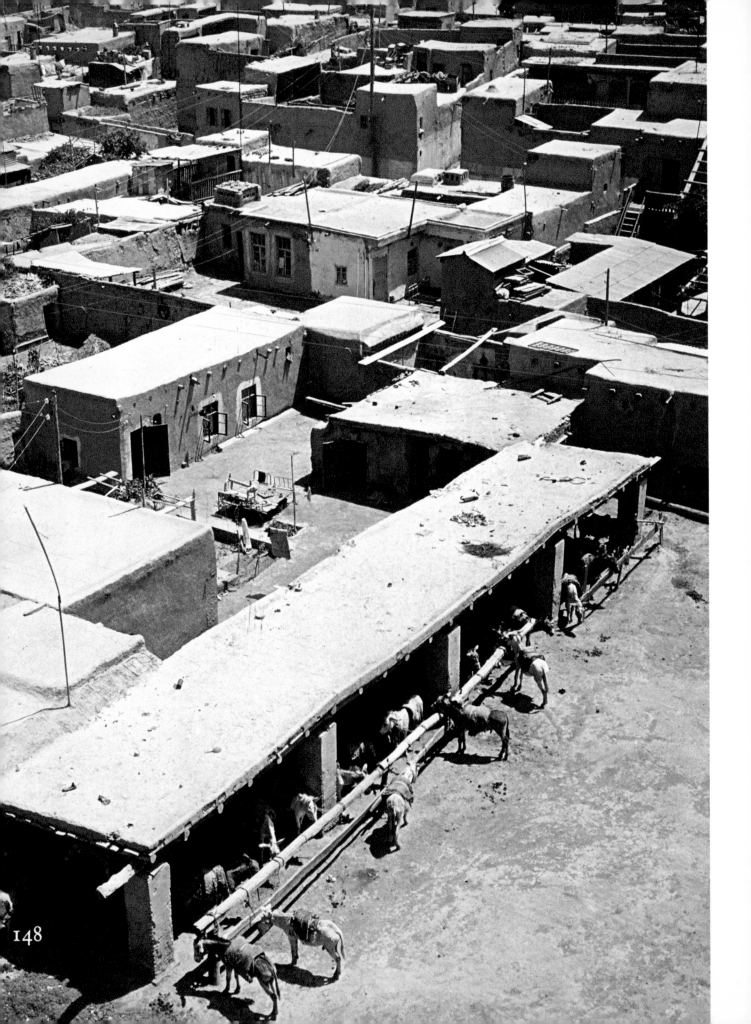

Russia is Rich

*Pages 146/147:
Left: The director
of a tobacco factory
in Tashkent.
Beside him the
indispensable abacus.
Middle:
Folksinger in Alma-Ata,
accompanying himself
on the Domra.
Right:
Men's business outside
an Uzbek tea-house.*

*Page 148:
View of a quarter of
the old city of Bokhara
where oriental flat roofs
cover the single-storey
white-washed clay
or stone buildings.*

*Page 149:
Street market in the old
Uzbek city of Samarkand,
once the capital of the
realm of Tamburlaine
who, from here, conquered
India, Persia, Asia Minor
and a large part
of Russia.*

*Page 150:
One of the mosques of
Samarkand, enchanting
in the wealth and beauty
of its ornamentation.*

...rich in her great size, her great beauty. Mountains, woods, steppes, rivers, pastures, she has them all on an enormous scale. Here are a few examples.

The Volga. Mother Volga.

In fact one might say: step-mother Volga. I travel downstream on a steamer. On the right bank where the mountains stand, the golden crosses of churches used to flash, illuminating like lighthouses the gloomy forests. Today they have almost totally disappeared. And the Volga too is not the same any more. It has been broken up into enormous reservoirs (Tybinsk, Moscow, Gorky, Kubyshev and Volgorod reservoir). Beneath their waters lie many hundreds of villages. In the old days one could sail from the upper course to the mouth in the delta of Astrakhan, and the banks would be piled with watermelons, sweet melons and fish.

Tsaritsyn. Later it became Stalingrad. Today one calls it Volgograd. A town of destiny. It grew, matured, and continued to look on its masters with a dark, lowered glance. The banks of the Volga have changed beyond recognition. Everywhere there are huge factories, drilling-towers, coal-mines, thousands of tractors working the steppes.

Russia's forests reach from ocean to ocean, guard the country from the banks of the Baltic to the bays of the Pacific Ocean, on the hills of Gruzinskaya and on the craters of the Far East volcanoes. The forests represent gigantic stores of wood, and they shelter innumerable fur-bearing animals. Year after year business people from all over the world come to the old house on the Moscow Prospect in Petersburg where valuable Siberian furs are auctioned, the most beautiful sable and ermine pelts, mink, the dream of all elegant women, silver and blue fox, golden and light-silver Persian lamb. All these valuable furs, which bring in the State colossal sums, are trophies of Siberian hunters unsurpassed in their bravery, endurance and mastery. For months they live hundreds of miles from home in the impenetrable Taiga, often desolate country that no man has ever entered. The hunter sets off from on a heavy sleigh having put himself into the care of St. Nicholas the Miracle-worker. His wife has put an enormous pack of *Pelmeni* (meat-filled pastries made of unleavened dough) into the sleigh. The monotonous sound of the bells accompanies him, as it says in the song, the roar of the gale in the tops of ancient spruce trees, and also the howling of hungry wolves—many a hunter has met his fate dozing off to become the prey of a pack of wolves. Even today such things happen. I have often met them, sitting around their camp fire in a clearing in the Taiga with the aroma of home-made Pelmeni tickling the appetite.... In the old days the hunters and the fur dealers lived 151 well. But today their hard profession brings in little, and I wondered why they didn't give it up. A hunter living in the Altai answered: 'Are you going to stop writing poems even if you aren't paid anything for them?'

The East begins at the Urals. They are gigantic. By European standards one can compare this region with a large country. Its climate is typically Russian with great variations in temperature, icy winters and dry, hot summers, and those wonderful autumns which 'enchant the eye' when in the southern areas the leaves glow in all the colours of the rainbow. The southern Urals are especially picturesque. Driving along the Bela, that torrent which only in its lower reaches becomes tame enough for ships to use its broad waters, driving from Magnitogorsk to Beloretsk through mountain forests, the splendid scenery is a rare delight. Heavy old trees provide pleasant shade, the rivers refresh and revive. Here one still comes upon villages of the heretic Old Faith with their houses of prayer and with broad-shouldered, full-bearded ancients looking like Emelyan Pugatchov.

From earliest times the Urals have been Russia's forge. At the time of Peter the Great, the Demidovs, Russia's first industrialists, began to produce iron and steel here. Since mineral coal was then unknown, the ore was smelted with charcoal. The charcoal burners and tar makers lived in forests. Old factories from that time, like the Beloresk, remain even now. Every kind of treasure to be found underground lies under the Urals. Their precious stones are unique. The halls of the Winter Palace and the Hermitage in Petersburg are decorated with wonderful malachite from this region. The domes of the Petersburg cathedrals shine with their gold. Rings, necklaces and diadems worn throughout the world sparkle with their sapphires, rubies, emeralds, aquamarine, topaz, onyx, beryl, amethyst and garnet.

One can find every type of coal in the Urals, also rich ore and copper mines, mercury and lead, tin and zinc, sulphur and asbestos, gold, silver and platinum.

These mineral resources form the raw materials of many industries. Here hundreds of different types of machines and instruments are manufactured. The Urals factory for heavy machinery which produces the equipment of whole heavy-industry factories and drilling apparatus, is Russia's largest industrial undertaking. From cars, electric locomotives and aeroplanes to small electrical motors, almost everything is manufactured here. And yet the careful observer will realize immediately that the most important thing, expert organization, sensible, unbureaucratic planning, is lacking. Many defective goods and obsolete, useless equipment are produced while on paper the production schedules are fully implemented.

While Yermak conquered Siberia, Russian explorer-generals found their way, in the south, to the Pacific Ocean. Yerofy Khabarov discovered the wealth of the Far East. The enormous Khabarovsky province, which is larger than France, bears his name.

After decades of exploration and enormous trouble, a road through the northern ice sea was discovered. But only the building of a considerable fleet of ice-breakers with an atomic ice-breaker at its head has produced a final solution of this enormous task.

The high north was explored, the Tundra, the underground mineral deposits north of the Arctic circle, and finally the Arctic itself. There are always expeditions, on floating stations, at work in the Arctic. In the Antarctic, in the settlements of

Mirny and Vostok, research projects are in progress, and the whaling fleets 'Slava' and 'Ukraina' kill thousands of whales and sperm-whales. Fur animals are hunted on the islands of the Arctic Ocean and in the Taiga. The inhabitants of the Tundras keep reindeer herds and hunt seals and walruses.

The north provides the country with many valuable goods. Beside the priceless furs, the products of reindeer herds and the sealfat, fishing produces ten thousand tons of herrings, cod and perch. These fish are one of the Russians' staple foods.

Travelling by express from Sverdlovsk to Vladivostok, one's impressions are dominated by the great variation in the landscape. After Tomsk there are hundreds of miles of steppes, Kulunda, Barabinskaya, endless. Around the station called 'Taiga', the steppes change slowly to the thick forests of the Taiga. This is middle Siberia. North of the trans-Urals there is still tundra, then begin the impenetrable forests of Tyumen. Not so long ago this far and lonely country suddenly made its voice heard: here the much-hoped-for Siberian petroleum was found. Abundant oil wells began to gush in the province of Tyumen.

Novosibirsk, the most important town and considerable industrial centre of Siberia, is going through a period of stormy growth. Its population has passed the million mark. The city lies on the Ob, one of the many gigantic rivers of Siberia with huge energy potential. Recently the Ob has been dammed to form a huge lake and a power station has been constructed. Here the largest West Siberian iron and steel works with a closed production cycle is being created.

Novosibirsk is also a centre of learning. There is a University, an Institute of Technology, and one of the most important centres of the Academy of Sciences with fifteen research institutes.

Kuznetsky, which boasts one of the largest steel factories in the country, has also grown, and so has Rubtsovsk, the coal centre of the Kuznetsky basin, the capital of the Altai province, one of the most important newly-settled districts. The problem of the newly-settled lands is unsolved today. A hundred million acres of this land have not increased the grain output of the country noticeably, in spite of enormous investments. The 'long rouble' (slang for higher pay) hoped for by so many has quickly proved to be a myth, not least since life in the Siberian cold, living in badly constructed barracks with inadequate diet, has proved almost intolerable. A general flight from these new settlements has begun.

In Siberia and Kazakhstan, the largest newly-settled districts, the corn ripens late, during the second half of September. It must therefore be reaped and stored in record time. But the necessary harvesting machines and transport were lacking, and, most of all, a sufficient labour force. The Government decided on compulsory duty by workers and later, even students, from the whole country. Lorries from Moscow, Leningrad and other cities were sent. But the loss of already scarce transport facilities increased the general economic chaos. In spite of all emergency measures the whole wheat crop fell victim to the snow in the third year of the new settlement of the Altai region.

The whole campaign remained a failure. After three, four years, the yield diminished catastrophically since the soil was soon short of lye and neither chemical nor natural fertilizer was available in large enough quantities. It reached the point where one had to buy grain with hard dollars from Uncle Sam. And yet Russia had produced six **153** hundred million *pood*** of grain through three centuries without tractors or machines, with only the help of the hand plough and the magic horse Sivka-Burka.

Even the example of the 'Hungry Steppes' of Central Asia cannot balance such failures. There a considerable part of the steppes, covering over twenty five million acres, has been transformed since the Second World War into cattle pastures and fields by building canals and digging for surface water.

But Siberia is not blessed with fruitful earth. Its truly inexhaustible wealth lies in its mineral resources (in Koluma alone, in Eastern Siberia, great seams of gold were removed), and in its forests (half the trees in the world are rooted in Siberia). The reserves of energy of the great Siberian streams are enormous: the Ob, Irtysh, Angara, Yenisey, Lena and Amur. But its industrial and economic development is hindered by the shortage of labour and the paucity of the population. Ten times as many people could live here, but in this rugged landscape covered in primeval forest there are too few towns and settlements.

IN SIBERIAN COLD

Page 155:
Kolkhos near Novosibirsk.
The 20th century has
conquered the Siberian
settlements.

Pages 156/157:
Huge steel works in
Kuznezk. Here and in
Magnitogorsk
the largest steel mills
of the Soviet Union are
situated.

Page 158:
Seal hunters on the shores
of the White Sea.

Page 159:
Hunter in the tundra
of northern Siberia.
The lives of these men of
Mongol extraction are
incredibly frugal,
tough and healthy.

Page 160:
Siberia is still a paradise
for wild bears,
for the West the symbolic
animal of Russia.

Page 161:
The small Siberian horses
are world-famous.
Their shaggy coats protect
them against the cold
which often reaches
sixty degrees of frost.

* A unit of weight, equal
to 36 lb. avoirdupois.

156

The Peasant and His Land

It is perhaps more true for Russia than for any other country that she can only develop peacefully when the question of her peasants and her agriculture has been settled satisfactorily. For a country with, today, approximately two thousand six hundred million acres of cultivated land, agriculture is still the decisive factor in the social structure. And Russia has been from ancient times an agricultural country*.

The peasant's attitude to his work is not the basic weakness in Russia's agricultural system. The peasant loves the Russian soil. When, under the Tsar, he conquered new lands, then his aim was to plough them.

Khlebopashets, (plougher of grain) was one of the names for the peasant, the husbandman; and *khleb* (bread, grain) was his most valuable commodity. The word became a synonym for wealth. 'Bread and Salt' became deep symbols of hospitality.** When the landed proprietor came from town to his estate, the peasants welcomed him with 'bread and salt', they met him carrying a loaf of bread and some salt in a cloth richly embroidered with traditional designs. (Krushchev, anxious to establish his popular image, introduced this friendly custom once again.)

The peasant's fundamental Christian feeling creates in him an almost mystical love for bread and grain. The last supper! Our daily bread! Since earliest times the Russian name for peasant has been Krestyanin, and thus the Christians were called in earlier centuries. Even in our time, there are peasants who, in times of great drought, pray to God for rain on their fields....

In the Podmoskovy, one is conscious of the nearness of Mother Russia in the villages and little towns, wherever one lives in the manner of peasants. In the morning the herdsman cracks his whip to wake up the peasant's wife so that the cows and goats can be milked and driven to pasture. Smelling of damp dust they make their way serenely to the forest clearing where they graze all day and go to drink at a small stream or pond. At night, when they return to the farmyard, you can hear the mooing of cows through the whole district. On the small terraces and in the entrances to houses, samovars are already steaming, families sit at their modest suppers, and in the distance boys and girls dance to the accordion.

People travel great distances to worship at the few remaining churches. And everywhere the old customs of the church feasts have been preserved. Every village has its own saint, and his name day is the feast day of the village. On this day almost nobody works, they sit together drinking their illicitly distilled vodka. All night long gay songs are sung until the first cock crows.

Page 162:
Here on the Angara River, near the new Siberian town of Bratsk, the largest hydro-electric plant in the world is being built.

* In 1861, 88 per cent of the population were peasants; in 1966 45.5 per cent.

** *Khlebossoly* (bread and salt) means 'hospitable person'.

Podmoskovy is lovely in the spring, the summer and the early autumn when the purple and gold aspen and birches glow in the evening light, when the traveller rejoices at the sight of the colourful leaves in the clearings in the wood, and the stubble fields glow a golden yellow. This magical time is only too short. Often there are still frosts in May, destroying the cherry and apple blossom, and in October the first snow falls. In former days, sleigh rides were organized in the winter, especially at Christmas and during the butter week, the Russian carnival. Exquisitely the snow creaked under the hooves, and the bells on the painted harness tinkled gaily. The housewives prepared mountains of pancakes, all the relations got together, one drank and ate, drank again, ate again, and one might eat a good half hundred of the delicious pancakes in a single evening. Then tea would be offered round and a towel passed round to wipe the sweat from one's forehead.

In the year 1861 the Government under Tsar Alexander II hesitantly began to make a first attempt at land reform. The law ending serfdom tried, of course, to spare the feelings of the landowners as much as possible. They retained the best properties. The freed peasants were given nothing. If they had money they could buy, if not, the village community *(mir)* farmed on lease. Only with its consent could a peasant move to another place. In some places the farming community organized a rota among families to work the better and worse pieces of land; in others the land leased by the village community was divided into equal parts for all the inhabitants. Thus everybody got a bit of pasture, a piece of good and a strip of bad land, which made rational working of the soil impossible. But the 'reform' of Alexander II did not in the least appease the land hunger, indeed it exacerbated it. The Russian peasants divided their property on the principle of justice equally amongst their sons without favouring the first-born, so that even after just one generation, a minimum subsistence could not any more be guaranteed. The Government did nothing for a long time to remedy this situation, until, in the Nineties, emigration to uninhabited Siberia became possible.

After the Revolution of 1905 Minister Stolypin took up the peasant problem. Every peasant was now allowed to move about, independent of his *mir,* and it was planned that he should have an entire piece of land as his property instead of the scattered fragments. By 1914 over a quarter of the country was turned into the private property of some of the peasants. It only seemed a matter of time before there would be the realization and consolidation of a just system of property ownership.

But the Bolsheviks obviated this. When, thanks to the rural population, they had won the civil war, they began to promote the idea of collectivism. By merging estates and collectivizing machines on the one hand, millions of peasants were to be made available to industry, while on the other hand Communist life in the *Kolkhos** would drum into the heads of the peasants with their bourgeois attitudes, the consciousness of a *classless society.* Could such a prospect fill people with enthusiasm who had just acquired their own land? Could the regime expect the peasants to be glad to renounce their new freedom?

In 1929 Stalin staged the 'Kolkhos Revolution' which is no less important than the Revolution of 1917. It was certainly not as bloodless as Soviet historians would have us believe. Especially in the south, in the Cossack settlements on the Don and Kuban it became a real civil war. Only a massive annihilation of the population, or

* *Kolkhos.* Collective economy; collective agricultural undertaking with collective responsibility by the Kolkhos peasants.
Sovkhos. State undertaking in which the agricultural workers are employed by the State and as such have no interest in its success.

164

exile in the far north, enabled the Communists to put down the insurrection. Day and night trains carrying exiles left the Ukraine, Don and Kuban at that time. Whole settlements, including old people and babies, were deported. They were taken to the deserted wastes of the Taiga where they were unloaded and left to their fate. They had to build shelters without tools or food, often in freezing cold. The overwhelming majority perished miserably. Whereupon the peasants all over Russia slaughtered their cattle, even their horses and their fowls. They refused to plough and to sow and the 'organized' famine of the Thirties killed more than a million people.

This happened in Europe in the twentieth century, because love of freedom and Communism were incompatible to the rural population. When, in the Forties, the responsible ministry fixed the fruit tax at treble the proceeds of the fruit harvest, and persisted in this absurdity, the fruit growers destroyed all the trees in their orchards. In 1965 the Soviet press, which does not usually paint a black picture, reported that only an insignificantly small proportion of the fruit trees had been replaced.

In the Soviet agricultural practice there are episodes which I have myself witnessed. Here are two grains of sand from a desert full of similar and worse examples....

Once I arrived late at night at a Sovkhos. As I drove along the fence I saw by the dim light of a lantern, held by a man in a torn jacket, two other men busily demolishing with sledge-hammers an absolutely new, heavy caterpillar tractor. I stopped the car to see what was going on. When I reached the people, they looked at me suspiciously. I was used to that. In the Soviet Union people are suspicious and every stranger is regarded as a spy. I showed my press card and asked in a cold but polite voice what was going on. One of those present, the head mechanic of the Sovkhos explained, looking darkly all around: 'Look, comrade correspondent, all Sovkhos and machine-tractor stations have to deliver a certain amount of old metal. In case of non-fulfilment of this order, the director of the undertaking is threatened with notice and exclusion from the Party. But unfortunately our tractor-maintenance people look after the machines much better than in other places. And as a result no machine has broken down the whole of this year. A few days ago we received a letter threatening that our provisions would be cut off if we did not deliver the old metal within three days. So we have to destroy a fine tractor to satisfy the bureaucrats. We have written more than once that we have no old metal, I myself have gone to see the district management. But the manager said to me: "Don't play stupid. In every Sovkhos there are umpteen broken tractors, some people have fulfilled the demand for old metal three and fourfold, only you are such magicians that you don't have anything!" So now we have to smash up this tractor.'—'But it's criminal!' I said.—'Comrade,' the mechanic said with a nod, 'our whole life is criminal. The Sovkhos makes a loss of two millions a year with this soil, that is worse than a smashed tractor.'

On another occasion I was again travelling in the Urals. This time I went to see the administration of an agricultural district. There I was received by the First Agronome. In spite of his high office, he was a young man of about twenty-five years. When I asked him how he liked the work he waved the question away with resignation and said in a sad voice: 'What do you mean work! I came here full of hope thinking, with a big enterprise, here's where one can achieve something. The manager fetched me from the station and told me that the chair in my office had only three legs, the fourth was broken, and there wasn't a workman who could repair it. I said to him: "I don't need your chair, I'm not an office drudge, I am an Agronome, I'm not here to sit around, my place is in the fields." He laughed. When we reached the administrative offices we met the director and I told him too that my place was in the fields. He also laughed and said that there were urgent letters from the Ministry of Agriculture for me to answer. There were about fifty such letters. All had to be answered immediately, any delay was threatened with every punishment in heaven and earth. But do you think a single one of those letters made any kind of sense? I won't bore you, but just look at this rubbish. It is the form for the quarterly statement of accounts. There are eighty-two points most of which are totally idiotic. For example: "How many mouselike rodents can be found in each of the Sovkhos and Kolkhos per square of the map, and what is the approximate number of plants that they destroy? How many vines and of what kind are raised in the district and how much is their approximate yield?" (What kind of vine would there be in the Urals, I ask you?) And there are many such questions. I was completely bemused, and worried endlessly in this ocean of forms. Then, one day, an inspection brigade invaded our Sovkhos—they never honour us with an inspection but come only to eat and drink at our expense—I turned to one of the inspectors with the request that he help me answer one of the quarterly forms. He simply laughed at me and advised me to put down any old figures, since nobody at the ministry would read the accounts in any case. They simply went straight into the archives. Why then this unproductive scribbling, you'll ask. To keep the millions of employees busy. And so I've never been able to get to the fields, but spend my time making out statements of accounts for the archives,' the young Agronome ended sadly.

The fact remains, it was a Utopian dream to try to educate the peasant into a classless agricultural worker and 'builder of communism'. For the work of the peasant is *creative work*. The Russian peasants have proved it since time immemorial.

WITHIN
THE POLAR CIRCLE

Page 167:
*Large parts of Siberia,
lying in the Polar regions,
are deserts of snow in which
sledges pulled by huskies
are the only means of
transport.*
*These regions are being
systematically explored,
since parts of them hold
great mineral deposits.*

Pages 168/169:
*Herds of reindeer in the
tundra. The reindeer
is related to the red deer.
In the tundra, where it feeds
mainly on moss, it is used
as a draught animal and for
riding, for its milk
and for its meat, and only
due to the reindeer is
human life possible in
these desolate regions.*

Democracy? Socialism?

It is very much in accordance with the Russian character that 'democracy' and 'socialism', those fascinating concepts, should have been the rallying cry of the political opposition and the intellectual avant-garde: the Social Democrats*, the Social Revolutionaries, and the Liberals who first united in the Kadet party.

One might have thought that the radical elements would have learned a lesson from the cruelly avenged December Revolt of 1825. Instead, the intelligentsia 'fought' on full of idealism against the autocracy, shaking away at the throne without noticing that they were weakening the Russian State. When, in 1881, a student assassinated Alexander II, it was not the autocracy but the Tsar's will towards liberalization that was eradicated. The reactionary measures of Alexander III following the murder did not advance the country one bit. Russia's defeat in the Crimean war (1854 to 1856) and the no less ignominious defeat in the Russo-Japanese war of 1904-5 are examples of the effects of internal weakness on foreign policy.

The demands of the opposition for a parliamentary government, land reforms, and new laws for industry were supported at the beginning of the 20th century by strikes and demonstrations. But the Minister of the Interior of that time, Pleve, believed that a 'successful small war' (in the East) was the magic charm that would raise the standing of the Tsar and bring peace and order back to the domestic scene. But even before the humiliating peace with Japan was signed, the first Revolution broke out in 1905. The Social Revolutionaries and the Social Democrats were in their element. But strikes alone do not make a Revolution, and there were no inflammatory slogans in the Opposition Party programme. Democracy? Universal suffrage? Well and good. But for what kind of Russia? In October the Social Democrats appointed the first workers' and peasants' councils (Soviets), a start towards a revolutionary government. The State Police soon dealt with that situation. The Revolution foundered because its supporters were incapable of formulating an inspired political programme. It was purely due to the risings and 'land conquests' of the peasants, which became more and more frequent towards the autumn, that the Government agreed to a compromise, finally granting the people, in the October Manifesto, the institution of the Duma, which was to be appointed by a general election—though the peasants wanted land rather than a parliament. In the first Duma, which met in the Taurida Palace in Petersburg in 1906, the Liberals had a majority of seats and threw themselves joyously into parliamentary activities. Unfortunately they were not allowed to get on with the business of government, and in the twelve years of its existence, the Duma never developed into a properly functioning parliament. Time

Page 170:
Two reindeer herdsmen in front of their summer tent in the far north of Yakutia.

* The Social Democrats split over a question of party politics in 1903 into *bolsheviki* and *mensheviki,* the majority and the minority.

171

was too short for it to function successfully, especially since the reactionary right and the extreme left obstructed it constantly.

The left couldn't, after all, agree to a constitutional monarchy! And their failure in 1905 had taught them that, beside the support of the industrial workers, they must at all costs mobilize that of the country population. Their moderate colleagues in the Opposition, on the other hand, had learned nothing nor would the Tsar listen to reason. He took refuge in paragraph 87 of the statute which gave him the right 'in case of need' to resume absolute power and to eliminate the Duma. After Russia had been brought into the war in 1914, the internal crisis smouldered on, but neither the Duma nor the local land and town administrations were allowed to develop their initiative to alleviate the precarious economic position. As democratic establishments they were a danger to the autocratic throne, and it was best to tie their hands in any case. In the meantime the monster Rasputin, a dissolute from Siberia who pretended to be a healer and holy man, and who was venerated by the Tsar and Tsarina, made his influence felt at Court. When, in the autumn of 1915, Tsar Nicholas II took over the general command at the Front, Rasputin in Petersburg named and dismissed ministers as the mood took him. All too late (at the end of December 1916), he was put out of the way of doing harm.

In the meantime the country's supply difficulties increased. The unhappy war situation worsened visibly, since the Russian soldiers were inadequately equipped. (One remembers the plea 'that since the English do not clean their rifles with bricks, we might be allowed not to clean them with brick either', never cleared the bureaucratic hurdles to reach the sovereign, whereupon the Crimean war was lost.)

This time more was lost. In February 1917* hunger and misery amongst the people solidified into Revolution. This was the hour of the Duma: as democratic representative of the will of the people it set up a provisional Government. The revolutionary *soviets,* workers' and soldiers' councils, who had established themselves in another wing of the Taurida palace, supported the Duma on the understanding that a general election would be called to set up a constituent assembly. The provisional Government accepted this as its first task. According to the democratic rules of the game, land reforms could only be carried through afterwards. In the meantime the peasants expropriated their masters off their own bat. In hordes they came back from the Front, so as not to get the worst of the bargain. At the same time the provisional Government was supposed to conduct a successful domestic and foreign policy. In the summer Lenin appeared from exile and began to work against the Government (whose Prime Minister that autumn was Kerensky) and to work also against the Social Revolutionaries and the Mensheviks. By blindly practising its democratic principles, the Government tolerated the open activities of those who were digging its grave. In October**, an All-Russian Congress of Soviets was to take place, and the Bolsheviks had chosen that day for their *coup d'Etat.* There was hardly any resistance! And now Lenin stood at the head of the new Bolshevist Government (Soviet of the People's Commissars). He knew well how to carry the Russian people along with him by assigning to them a mission encompassing the whole world: *workers of the world unite!* A second fundamental slogan of the October Revolution sounded no less sublime, and was assured success by its timeliness: *world-wide 'democratic' peace!* And Russian arms were turned no longer on the Germans. It was thus that the rumour was

Stolypin (1863 to 1911) took over the Tsarist Ministry of the Interior in 1906 and after only a few weeks was appointed President of Ministers by the Tsar.
He was an inexorable and ruthless opponent of the Revolutionary Left. During his time in office over four thousand five hundred death sentences were carried out, some through special courts. The hangman's rope became commonly called 'Stolypin's necktie'.

* By the Julian calender. By the Gregorian calender, or New Style, on 8th March.

** Old Style 25th October, New Style 7th November. The New Style, which is used everywhere, was introduced in 1918.

created that the German Kaiser had transferred to the Bolsheviks fifty million in gold.

But only one thing could bring the Bolsheviks the complete support of those peasants who still comprised the vast majority of the people: *all the land for the peasants!* With Machiavellian ingenuity, Lenin put this promise at the head of his programme. In this way Lenin hoped to make the 'proletarian, exploited masses' happy and content, but the 'Whites' now began to resist. Civil war raged worse than the Tartars ever had.... It was fought so bitterly and cruelly because both sides were convinced of their cause (unlike the Civil War in the United States where the moral factor gave the North a psychological advantage), and because neither side could see the point of view of the opponent. Both staked everything on a just and sacred mission: to save Russia.

He tried to counter revolutionary agitation by a land reform which, while ameliorating the economic position of some of the peasants, made the misery of the majority worse. In this way the country proletariat were forced into a common cause with the industrial proletariat of the cities, a phenomenon later used by Lenin with much success. On 14th September 1911 Stolypin was assassinated during a Gala performance of the Kiev Opera.

'Classless' Society

Lenin had a slogan in his repertoire: 'We will build lavatories of gold!' For every single worker, of course. Symbolizing the Communist paradise.

For half a century the Russian people drudged under enormous deprivations to build this paradise. Those who didn't want to help with the building, or who became suspicious, were not worthy of the golden future and were liquidated.

The golden gleam of a distant paradise has gone. The people want to live. For fifty years they have been queueing interminably for a decent life. It doesn't have to be of pure gold, but it has to be life. Now!

The people begin to grumble and to scold. Not only because they have only the most scanty necessities of life, but because they live so very much *not* in paradise.

Soviet propaganda is always boasting that so many houses are built in the Soviet Union. And indeed, not a little building goes on. But how? The majority of the new blocks consist of one- and two-room flats. There are hardly any larger flats, and these are usually given to some influential bureaucrat. One has hardly moved into such a flat when it becomes as confined as a communal flat. In many of our cities two families are once again living in most of the two-room flats, often the married son or daughter lives in it as well. And so there is once again dirt, wrangling, abuse, and disputes about the single cooking-ring.

Even the Soviet press has been publishing articles saying that building is slow, expensive and bad. Yet even these flats, or as one says in the Soviet Union, 'living areas', are objects for dreams and years of waiting. There are still families today who have to wait ten or fifteen years for a one-room flat. In the meantime they have a room in a communal flat. And quite incredible things can happen, as, for example, the following case: a couple were divorced, whereupon both parties remarried. But they continued to live, each with their new partner, still in their one room, separated only by a thin screen.

Hundreds of thousands of families still vegetate in crooked little wooden shacks without water, drainage, or heating. At the beginning of 1966, in Moscow alone more than thirty thousand such tumble-down shacks still existed.

And why is it like that? Because the Soviet power makes great promises that it does not keep, that it cannot keep.

For the women of Russia life is even harder to bear than for the men. Since they have completely equal rights, they have to bear the same enormous burdens as the men, as well as their housewifely duties. That means six *full* days of work a week as crane driver or dredger driver, as overworked doctor, on building sites (the over-

Under Alexander II who reigned from 1855 to 1881 and who, despite a certain liberal outlook, could not rouse himself to institute a constitutional government, the activities of the Social Revolutionaries increased constantly. The Government took refuge in 'strong arm policies', there were arbitrary administrative deportations to Siberia. These acts of despotism were answered with acts of terrorism by the Social Revolutionaries. From 1878 there were

a number of unsuccessful attempts at assassination on the person of the Tsar. On Sunday, 13th March 1887 he took part in a military march-past. On the return journey, beside the Catherine canal, Grinevetsky threw the bomb that killed the Tsar. The effect was frightful. Both the Tsar's legs were shattered, and about twenty people, among them the would-be assassin himself, lay dying or badly wounded in the street. (Contemporary woodcutting.)

whelming majority of building workers are women), or as teachers (having to teach the children the Party line). The amount of work they do is obligatory, the regime demands it, and apart from this even the smallest family could not exist without the woman's pay. On the seventh day (it is not called Sunday, but the day off) she cannot go out but scrubs and washes and mends. Where are the ideals for which they have endured and suffered for fifty years? What a monstrous discrepancy between ideal and reality....

What a difference between the ordinary people and the Party bosses and bureaucrats, who prosper in the meantime! They have everything that a Soviet citizen could wish for (apart from the certainty that they'll still be in their post tomorrow).

They have country houses at their disposal, limousines with chauffeurs, larger flats, privileged shopping facilities and dispensaries.

Social problems have always been serious in Russia. At the beginning of the 18th century only 8 per cent of the population was literate, 92 per cent lived in extreme simplicity, unenlightened, as serfs. The élite, in the meantime, enjoyed culture and 'good taste'. The aesthetic, sometimes merely sumptuous style of life of the noble classes is well known from our literature, but the social endeavours and the poverty of the majority were also immortalized, especially during the 19th century.

The Soviet regime follows, as once did the Tsarist empire, the course towards greatness. Military parades, sputniks and its foreign policy are supposed to symbolize this greatness. The State doesn't care how the people live. Klyuchevsky, the greatest Russian historian of the 19th century, once said: 'The State grows fat, the people pine away....'

An evil that can be diagnosed should be capable of remedy, one might think....

Sputniks Instead of Safety Razors

On the 22nd of January 1905 a huge workers' demonstration took place in Petersburg.
A procession of 140,000 unarmed people, workers with their wives and children, marched to the Winter Palace, the residence of the Tsar. The demonstrators carried pictures of the Tsar, holy pictures and church banners. During the march they sang hymns. The object of the demonstration was to hand to the Tsar a petition signed by 135,000 people. It said: 'We, the workers of the city of Petersburg, our wives and children and helpless ancient parents, have come to you, Gosudar, to seek justice and protection. We are made

According to statistics the Soviet Union is today the second greatest industrial power in the world. It is characteristic of Soviet philosophy that the State's investment and production policy is not geared to the needs of the population but to the furthering of the prestige of the Party and the State. At the time when the Soviet Union was the first country in the world to put a sputnik into space, and on account of this technological achievement was admired and envied by everyone, it was practically impossible to buy a safety razor. In a word: despite the high standard of technological development, the production of consumer goods left much to be desired, both in quantity and quality. That is why, by western standards, the people are poorly dressed. Wages are so low, that the purchase of a coat or suit present great problems. A good quality garment is very expensive, its price approximately twice the monthly wage of a worker or employee. Such a sum can only be saved by going without necessities. I have known many people who for years never ate any butter, never went to the theatre, never went away on holiday, so as to buy themselves something new. Furniture is exorbitant. A reasonable set of living room furniture costs more than a thousand roubles, that is about as much as the annual wage of a Soviet employee! But even if one has the money, it is difficult to buy good quality goods. Ready-made clothes are made coarsely from old-fashioned models. Shoes are of miserable quality. And yet one needs them badly, only a few cities have taxis, and the networks of buses are inadequate.

Even shopping is hard on the footwear, for everyone is looking for imported goods. But these are so rare, that one often spends months searching for a pair of imported shoes in the shops, or a nylon shirt or wool sweater. If one wants to buy a refrigerator one is first put on a waiting list—then one will get it in five years' time! In the last few years it has become almost impossible to buy a car. The first series of the Moskvitch cost 700 roubles, the second 2500 roubles, and the third 4711 roubles. Carpets are luxury articles in the truest sense of the word. Toilet soap, simple toilet soap, is not even manufactured in the Soviet Union: it is imported from East Germany. Anyone is prepared to pay several roubles for a simple western ball point pen. And hundreds of objects which are part of everyday life in the West, are unknown even in name to the Soviet citizen.

In 1967, the jubilee year of the October Revolution, the Soviet trade paper *Trood* published an open letter in which the director of an iron combine in Karaganda had a go at the Soviet trade minister. The supply situation in the neighbouring town of Temir-Tau (in the Soviet Republic of Kazakh) was beyond bearing, he said, there

were neither winter boots nor woollen dresses, and fruit and vegetables were equally scarce. In the winter and spring no potatoes (the traditional staple diet in Russia) were available. The town had a hundred and fifty thousand inhabitants, and there were only six hundred coats available for its twenty three thousand children, for the spring and autumn, even fewer for the winter. And that for the children, whose welfare in all the propaganda has always been written in capital letters. Temir-Tau is the most important oil centre of Central Asia, and its population consists chiefly of oil specialists and their families who, like all workers in heavy industry, belong to the top category for provisions. If they are looked after like that, how does the fourth category make out?

It is therefore not to be wondered at that a high official of the Gos Plan (State plan for production) confessed to me with a sad smile: 'Our consumer goods economy carries enormous losses, while the capitalists, even though they have no Gos Plan, take a great deal of notice of the demands of the population and produce goods that are much in demand, and therefore make great profits. And what is the point of hiding the fact that the quality of goods in capitalist countries is infinitely higher than ours? While most goods are scarce here, they have everything in super-abundance. The dreadful problem here are the idle employees. I believe that we in the Soviet Union have about ten million unnecessary employees. And the unfortunate thing is that they not only do not work themselves, but that they prevent other people from working. By asking for endless statements of accounts, they delay every single decision endlessly and send out thousands of unnecessary documents.'

I asked: 'Why don't you give the sack to the people you know are doing nothing?'

He laughed bitterly: 'Don't you understand that one can't just sack ten million people, people who can't do anything and don't want to do anything and who get a big wage as well? They'd stage a revolt. And in any case, these stubborn bureaucrats are the chief support of the Soviet power. And what would it look like to Europe? We are so proud of not only having no unemployment, but that we have too few workers. Of course we really do have too few workers, especially building workers. There are millions too few workers, but we have millions of idlers. And this situation cannot be altered. We have carried out so many reforms. How often have we set up new Ministries, or dissolved old ones. Krushchev's "reform" alone, dissolution of Ministries, Workers' Councils, Executive Committees and Party Committees cost several hundred million roubles. Now we are carrying out the opposite reforms, and that doesn't cost any less....'

For, imagine, Krushchev himself had, for a time, the desire to fight bureaucracy. Even he was horrified by the truly gigantic size of Soviet bureaucracy. According to his directions, the Central Committee of the Party therefore addressed a letter of instructions to all party organizations which contained the following example: A *kommunkhos* (management of a communal enterprise) in the provinces decided to sell a wagon and two horses to the consumer society of the same town. The price was agreed, but each sale of this kind has to be authorized by the Ministerial Council of the Republic. (Of course the enormous quantity of such trifles encumbers the agendas of the sessions of the Ministerial Councils of all national Republics unbearably, and causes months' delay in the authorization of local decisions.) Then the following happened: the groom decided that it was unnecessary to feed the horses particularly 177 well since they were anyway as good as sold. It would be better to save oats, especially since the budget had just been drastically cut. But the horses did not concur with the economic deliberations of those in charge of them, they got very thin, and one fine day they died. Soon after this the authorization for the sale arrived from the Ministerial Council of the Russian Federation of Soviet Republics. When someone from the consumer society came to collect the wagon and horses, he was told that the horses had given up the ghost. Law proceedings were instituted, and the inevitable question was asked: Who was to blame? Who paid the cost?

It goes without saying that nobody would dare to accuse the imperfect Soviet system, where seventy-seven people make decisions on every matter and in reality nobody is responsible. Everybody co-ordinates and co-ordinates, and at the end it's all Pushkin's fault, as the Russians say. When the law proceedings started, all parties washed their hands in innocence. The groom declared that the manager of the communal enterprise had told him to be sparing with the oats, the manager justified himself by saying that his estimated expenses had been cut. The manager of the consumer society declared he bore no responsibility for the power of resistance of the horses, also that he had no right to hurry up the Ministerial Council which had delayed the matter for more than four months. For about two years the proceedings were dragged through various courts, and only came to an end when the manager of the communal enterprise followed the example of the horses by giving up the ghost himself....

Of course life as such does not always and everywhere submit itself to such bureaucratic formalism. Odessa offers a typical example, Odessa, an amusing city which might be called the Russian Naples.

Odessa is really an individual State. It hasn't allowed even the Communists to get it down. If you ask a man from Odessa where he comes from, he will answer, especially if it is a foreigner asking the question, as follows: 'My home is Odessa-Mama, I am afraid of no one but God the Father, I don't give a hoot for the rest, especially the Tchekists.' In all Russia every restaurant closes at eleven. Except in Odessa. Not so very long ago I was in a restaurant in Odessa with some friends. When, at eleven o'clock, the waiter came with the bill, my friend looked at him and said: 'You know, my young friend, somehow I'm not in the mood to pay before two o'clock, and will you tell the musicians not to be in a hurry to go home, else they might meet with some unpleasantness on the way. That's all, my young friend, and I don't want to see your beautiful face again until two o'clock.'

The musicians remained. My friend ate three portions of Chicken à la Kiev. The musicians were polite enough to play everything we liked. To show our gratitude we sang. At three o'clock in the morning we continued to sing in the street. You should try some time to sing in the streets of Moscow or any other town. Immediately a 'Milton' would appear (this is the name Muscovites give their policemen), and he would say in a commanding tone: 'Come, citizen, stop that.' I was surprised that here no policeman came to see what we were up to, that in Odessa I had hardly seen a policeman. I asked my friend for an explanation and he told me: 'The police can't do a thing with the people of Odessa, and the people of Odessa can't do a thing with their police. We understand each other. If our young people want to have a bit of fun, our police become short-sighted. In any case, the Soviets seem to understand that the

History produced a figure at the end of the reign of the Tsars and of feudal society in whom all subterranean Russian forces had come together in devil's form. In the year 1907 the son of Siberian peasants, a tramp and horse thief, came through the good offices of various noble ladies to the court of the Tsar. Modestly he called himself 'Starez (Elder) Grigory'. Presumably he received the name Rasputin because of his dissolute life

people of Odessa aren't madly enthusiastic about Communism. The people of Odessa are individualists, not friends of the great masses, on the contrary, they love conviviality in small groups with good friends and jolly girls. Only the mice dance in our collective clubs.'

And because the police here close both eyes, there is the Odessa market. In this market one can buy anything: Japanese jackets, pipes from Singapore, a kangaroo coat from Sydney, ivory necklaces from Honolulu, the ginseng root from Hong Kong, medicines from Madras, nylon shirts from San Francisco, cocaine from Hamburg, yes, even a doctor's diploma and a foreign passport. Odessa is a city of scintillating character. It has more than a hundred factories and an important harbour. Russians live there and Greeks, Armenians, Jews and, yes, even Negroes. From early morning tens of thousands of people are at the bazaar. Odessa is the Café Franconi and blond Mishka (Isaac Babel's 'Benya Krik'). Odessa is a city of heroes and rogues. It knows how to preserve that much freedom.

Through the Eternal to the New

When one compares the half century of Soviet rule with the previous history of Russia, it looks like a distorting mirror reflecting the past. The Stalin era is like the time of Ivan the Terrible enlarged to grotesquely horrible proportions. There are many parallels, but increased a thousandfold, with the terror of the reign of Nicholas I.

Ivan the Terrible was Russia's first heartless tyrant. Above anything he loved the colour red. Red and beautiful became synonyms (in Russian *krasniy* and *prekrasniy*). On the day of his coronation the whole of Moscow, then still a town of wooden buildings, was decorated with red flags. Ivan went into battle with red flags, red was the colour of the scaffold and of the robe of the executioner. Ivan spared no one. He destroyed the Boyars, he suspected his closest advisers, especially after the freedom-loving Prince Kurbsky had risen against him. He murdered his son.... He imagined *every courageous person* to be his enemy. When the Metropolitan warned him of the consequences of his deeds, the Tsar ordered him: 'Be silent—and bless me.' The Metropolitan answered courageously: 'Our silence opens your soul to sin, and brings death.'

The people maintained an apathetic silence.

Nicholas I was also a hard dictator, but he at least was enlightened enough to cloak his arbitrary actions with the excuse of 'reasons of State'. His subjects also were more enlightened, they grumbled, they ventured to criticize Russia's spiritual climate, they even concerned themselves with ideas. And this after the Tsar had dealt so thoroughly with the insurgent Decembrists! In 1836 Tchaadayev published his 'Philosophic Letter to a Lady' in a journal, whereupon the editor was exiled, and the writer of this enormity was declared insane and put under police supervision. (Those were days when police still allowed such madmen, who did not recognize that theirs was the only true and valid government, to remain free.) True, 'reasons of State' soon made it necessary for the Tsar to assume other methods. In the early Forties of the last century some of those who endangered the State by taking part in liberal *discussion circles* were executed (among them Ryleyev, the poet), while others were exiled to Siberia (among them Dostoevsky). A bare hundred years later Nikolay Gumilev, Boris Kronilov, Ossip Mandelstam, Isaac Babel, Boris Pilnyak, Pavel Vassilev, Nikolay Sarudin suffered the same fate. Sergey Yesenin, Vladimir Mayakovsky, Marina Svetlayeva committed suicide.

Fifty years of Soviet rule. It is only an episode in the millenium of Russian history. For a generation is now growing up which is not paralyzed by the Terror any more, and who understand despite all direct and indirect propaganda that Russia did not

The industrialization of the Soviet Union is based on the natural wealth of the country which makes the importing of raw materials practically unnecessary. Despite the crippling bureaucracy, and despite the set-backs of the Second World War, the second largest industrial power has, in the course of one generation, risen out of a country ravaged and disorganized by war and a revolution.

*Page 181:
Today electronics are the deciding factor in the fate of every industrial power. Here girl workers are making electric steering equipment.*

*Page 182/183:
Grain harvest at a Sovkhos (State Enterprise) in the new districts of Kasakhstan.
The Kolkhos and Sovkhos were established despite the resistance of the peasants. Their aim is to industrialize agriculture as quickly as possible, and to free workers for industry.
Collectivization is an attempt to create, from the traditional peasant, a type of person whose whole feeling for life resembles that of an industrial worker.*

187

189

191

begin in 1917. The generation which took part in the Revolution and the Civil War judged the fate of Russia thus: the victorious Reds put all their strength and idealism into the building of a completely new nation, founded on the 'only true' concepts. Everything in the past, and that meant the bad, the spoilt, the worthless, was destroyed and overcome. The bright paradise lay ahead.

For the defeated Whites, on the other hand, for those circles which emigrated between 1917 and 1920 after they had lost their town and country houses and the very foundations of their lives to the Reds, everything in the past had been destroyed, and that meant everything holy, precious, great. Nothing was left of the true Russia. The anti-Christians raged, began systematically digging up the Russian roots and sowing Soviet weeds, cutting down everything that tried to grow over their garden fence. How many giant trees did they not cut down because they were taller than the average 'proletarian' plant....

But the Russian soul is still the same. Holy Russia continues to procreate the Russian spirit. The history of a thousand years does not vanish into thin air to please the Bolsheviks and sadden the emigrants. Russia's past, rich in courage and in tears, in ostentation and penury, is also a living factor in the present, and this fact in itself has in it the seeds of change of the Communist *idea*. On the other hand, the fact that the present-day Soviet system is based on a pseudo-religion brings with it of necessity the end of the existing Communist *practice*. They, the Communists, who called real religion 'the opium of the people' (because the Tsars had misused it for their own purposes), now use their 'religion' to lead the Russian people by the nose. But every misused religion, and indeed every ideology detached from the existing truth, will run itself into trouble in the end. The insurrections and strikes of the last years in Novocherkask and Tiflis, in Donbas, in Odessa and Mogilov, speak clearly and have successfully unmasked Communist malpractice. The Russian people cannot *live* on demagogy and promises for the future. The basis of a new Russia, real faith and the love of freedom, have remained within the people. They will lead the country to a new spring.

Pages 184/185:
As in other great cities, enormous changes are taking place in Moscow. In the city, high blocks of flats and skyscrapers spring up. Beyond a huge building site our picture shows the Hotel Ukraine which was built in 1956 in the style of the Stalin era. It is about 550 feet high and has a thousand rooms.

Pages 186/187:
Idyll from the past: an abandoned railway station in Grodno, a little town not far from the present Polish border.

Pages 188/189:
Gigantic workshop in an industrial enterprise in the Urals.

Pages 190/191:
Wood is one of Russia's greatest treasures. Along the rivers and streams it is floated to the places where it is used.

Page 192:
Vostok rocket by which the space capsule is put into orbit around the Earth. With such a rocket, cosmonaut Yuri Gagarin took off on 12th April 1961 to be the first man to travel in space. The rocket is approximately 120 feet long and develops a thrust of twenty million horsepower.

Russia's Hopes

In the second half of the 19th century, particularly in Petersburg and Moscow, there appeared a group of people who, in Russia, were called the 'Intelligentsia'. This should not be confused with the Western European 'Intellectuals', people engaged in intellectual creative work, especially scholars, writers, artists, university professors and pedagogues. People could belong to the Russian intelligentsia without having anything to do with those activities. As a social phenomenon, the intelligentsia recalls a religious order or sect. It had a strongly defined, very intolerant moral philosophy, a fixed view of life, it enforced its own habits and customs, and its members began to appear quite distinct in their outward appearance from other social groups. It was a group held together by ideological beliefs, recruited from various social classes, originally mainly from clerical circles, minor officials, petit bourgeois, and, after the abolition of serfdom, peasants. Most characteristic of the intelligentsia was their spiritual and social uprootedness, the break they made with all established customs and traditions. What made them into a sect was their dogmatism, a dogmatism favoured by a typical Russian trait: what, in the West, might be seen as scientific theory, as hypothesis or partial truth not demanding universal acceptance, easily becomes, for the Russian, rigid dogma. The Russian is also inclined to generalize every idea and make it into an absolute. The critical scepticism of the Western European does not suit him.

Thus the Russian intelligentsia came together under the banner of great ideals, and worked intensively for theories which promised great things. It was productive in its social criticism, and uncovered many diseases in the body politic. And yet it did not lead to anything. History has convicted this group of people of complete incompetence in finding practical solutions for its carefully deliberated and worked-out tasks. It produced no constructive activity at all.

Why was this? Was the obstacle our glorious but fatal inborn tendency for endless discussion amongst congenial people, or those with different ideas, without ever thinking of the demands of practical life? It is certain that the incompetence of the Russians as a whole and the Russian intelligentsia in particular, revealed itself in this way. Or did Russia, in its infinite spaces, its deep forests, its country seats around Moscow, its summer residences around Petersburg and on the banks of the Volga, did Russia give herself up to too many dreams? One dreamed a great deal about Russia's future, but one did little to put these dreams into execution. Or was the Russian intelligentsia perhaps too radical? It certainly never built a mighty State as did such statesmen as Peter the Great, or Catherine II.

194

On 1st December 1825 Tsar Alexander I died. He was the victor over Napoleon and co-creator of the 'Holy Alliance', that alliance which was supposed to stabilize the monarchies and conservative governments of the whole of Europe. Alexander I's successor, his brother Nicholas I, pictured above, continued his predecessor's policies, and in the first days of his reign put down the Decembrist revolt by force of arms. The object of the Decembrists, a group of young officers of the Russian nobility, 'infected' by Western ideas, was to transform Tsarist absolutism into a constitutional monarchy. After the speedy suppression of the rebellion, a special court passed many death sentences and sentences of banishment. In accordance with the 'Holy Alliance', the Polish revolution of 1830/31 was put down with much bloodshed, and in 1849 the Tsar intervened, at Austria's request, in Hungary, suppressing the national revolution there. The treaty which consisted of a preamble and three articles and which was signed in Vienna on 26th September 1815 by the Russian Tsar, the King of Prussia, and the Austrian Emperor, was called the 'Holy Alliance'. In the preamble, the three monarchs promised to base their government on the 'Immortal Religion of the Divine Redeemer'. The first article read: 'In accordance with Holy Writ which commands all men to consider themselves brothers, the three monarchs concluding this treaty are united by the bonds of a true and indissoluble brotherhood and, regarding each other as members of but a single country, will at every opportunity and in every place give each other support, assistance and help.'

We have never had a Franklin, that American intellectual who was one of the true founding fathers of America's nationhood. From the very beginning, our philosophers were followers of Voltaire, sceptics who undermined the spiritual strength of the Russian State. Let us look at the list of our thinkers: Tchaadayev, Radishchev, Novikov, Herzen, Bakunin, Kropotkin, Tchernishevsky, their attitude was biased against the State. Both the pre-Revolutionary intelligentsia, and the bourgeois youth of our own century were equally radical. The progressive intelligentsia of this time was alienated from reality. The philosophers who determined Russia's ideas thought little if at all of the Russian State. The philosophers Solovyov, Shestov, Berdayev, Bulgakov, Frank, Lossky, were as far removed from everyday Russia as were the great poets of that time: Alexander Blok, Andrey Bely, Anna Akhmatova, Nikolay Gumilov, and Sergey Gorodetsky. Not only the symbolists, but also those poets who tried to come to terms with reality, saw it as something exotic. They were seeking for a higher reality, and remained unsuspecting until suddenly confronted with nothingness. Perhaps this was also the reason why they proved incapable, when they had emigrated and were far from home, of building up an organization which could have fought actively for the democratic future of Russia.

And yet serious, urgent warnings were sounded, most clearly perhaps by Dostoevsky in his *Devils,* one of the most amazing works in the literature of the world. With staggering prophetic force Dostoevsky unmasked the revolutionaries as a band of adventurers and murderers. How tragically, and on what a huge scale this was corroborated at the time of Stalin, when the best people were murdered merely for remaining honest and refusing to be bought.

Pushkin and Dostoevsky were the greatest men of genius of the Russian spirit. They portrayed all the potentialities and peculiarities of the Russians. Both had grasped the spirit of both Russia and Europe. They *embodied* both Russia and Europe.

Pushkin was the first to put the Russian character and the Russian State under the magnifying glass, and in his great work he proved that he understood them intuitively. He wrote: 'It was probably the devil who prompted me, a person with intelligence and talent, to be born in this damned country.' Pushkin suffered within the society which destroyed him, but in exile he suffered *for* that society and for the Russian people. He is their mouthpiece.

As a young man, Dostoevsky made the exploration of the soul his aim and descended into the very depth of the Russian spirit. His whole work, his whole life were a great self-analysis and an analysis of the soul, an occupation with problems that did not seem to exist for the rest of the world, a search for the final answer to the 'damned questions' about human existence.

From my earliest years I have venerated Dostoevsky. There never was a greater poet, and perhaps nobody will ever equal him. Dostoevsky's destiny is the destiny of Russia. With Raskolnikov and Mitya Karamazov, yes, with the author himself, Russia went into exile in pathless Siberia. With Ivan Karamazov Russia went painfully seeking the way to God. And she took this road in the company of Alyosha Karamazov. With Fyodor Karamazov she caroused, shaken by low passions. The fate of Dostoevsky was a terrible and longed-for destiny, full of misfortune and bitter happiness, of hectic quests and despairing humility. All his heroes were in love with the tragic beauty of Russia and her women. Like his hero Prince Myshkin, the author

195

was driven mad by his desire to do some good in the cruel world of Yepantchins, Svidrigaylovs, Marmeladovs, the world of usurers and sinister figures. They fought their way from the hell of old Karamazov, the devils Pyotr Vershovensky, Stavrogin, Kirillov and Shatov, into the realm of God. And even today they are still on their way. Russia gave birth to this greatest of poets, and he in his turn created this inconceivable, half-mad, Holy Russia standing at the edge of the abyss. Dostoevsky is a Russian.... And that is perhaps our greatest honour and our greatest pride.

Dostoevsky foresaw Russia's unhappy fate not only because he had understood the Russian character, but also because he himself was, as it were in the highest degree, a Russian. He coined the phrase: 'Man gets used to anything, the low-down scoundrel....'

But servility has not got the better of all Russians. Great, shining examples of this are my friends Boris Pasternak and Alexander Yessenin-Volpin. Although their attitude brought them calumny and persecution, they remained true to themselves. Alexander Grin, long misjudged and banished, but always loved by the people, has at last, if only posthumously, gained long-deserved recognition in the Soviet Union. That too is a victory for the Russian people in their long ideological fight for freedom. One of the few writers in the Soviet Union who has succeeded in remaining an honest man is Constantin Paustovsky. But he had to renounce many things. I shall never believe that an artist of such talent left the broad, passionate high road to take the narrow path through the forest and write only about the beauties of nature in Russia. He understands better than anyone the heroic fight for freedom in which the people are engaged. I am deeply sorry that he remains neutral.

The poets are the mouthpiece of the intelligentsia, and they express what that part of society which is conscious of its responsibility feels. Their words are the weights on the delicate scales which measure the present and past of a people. Before my eyes the tall figure, the wonderful face of Alexander Blok arises, who bore such a tragic fate. He loved to roam aimlessly about the Nevsky Prospect, a Scythian who wrote the incomparable poem *The Scythians* in which he expressed the Russian longing for the union of all mankind, and begged the people of Western Europe to understand Russia:

. . . . .

Old world, before your ancient splendour sinks—
all-wise one, suffering sweet torment—
like Oedipus before the riddling Sphinx
pause and consider for a moment.

Russia is a Sphinx. Grieving, jubilant,
and covering herself with blood
she looks, she looks, she looks at you—her slant
eyes lit with hatred and with love.

Yes—love. For centuries you have not known
such love as sets our hot blood churning.

THE ARTIST

Art, poetry, theatre and music receive more State support in the Soviet Union than in any other country in the world. But the State expects the artist to commit himself and his work unconditionally to its aims. Artists who put the truth within their conscience above that of the regime find themselves in tragic conflicts. The regime tries to guard against the spiritually and artistically free by defamation of character, by committal to mental institutions, or by painful law proceedings followed by prison sentences.

*Page 197:
Boris Pasternak
(died 1960) and
Anna Akhmatova (left),
two outstanding
Russian poets
of the twentieth century.
Pasternak, who became
celebrated through his
novel Doctor Zhivago
was disgraced in the
Soviet Union, but has since
then been tacitly
rehabilitated. He has
earned the lasting gratitude
of Russian literature by his
large-scale Shakespeare
translations alone.*

*Page 198:
Scene from Mussorgsky's
opera Boris Godunov
being performed in the
Latvian State Theatre
in Riga. Even in provincial
theatres the artistic
standards are scarcely less
high than in Moscow.*

199

You have forgotten that the world has shown
love can devastate with its burning!

All things we love—the mystic's divine gift,
the fever of cold calculus;
all we appreciate—the Frenchman's shaft
of wit, the German's genius…

and we remember all things—hellhole streets
of Paris, cool Venetian stone,
lemon groves far off, fragrant in the heat,
and smoky pinnacles of Cologne.…

We love the flesh, its colour and its taste,
its suffocating mortal odour.…
Are we to blame if your rib-cages burst
beneath our paws' impulsive ardour?
. . . . .

Come to us—from your battlefield nightmares
into our peaceful arms! While there's
still time, hammer your swords into ploughshares,
friends, comrades! We shall be brothers!
. . . . .

Now, for the last time, see the light, old world!
To peace and brotherhood and labour—
our bright feast—for the last time you are called
by the strings of a Scythian lyre!

With the same ardour, Blok searched for the mysterious 'Unknown' which would bring him happiness. Full of anguish, he wrestled for a road to God for himself and for his friends, without ever really finding it. In the fevered dream of his last days he created the ballad *The Twelve* which has since become so famous. In this poem twelve Red Guards are patrolling the streets of bloodsoaked Petersburg on a winter's night during the time of the Revolution, shooting senselessly right and left. They feel that they are the tool of an unknown, anonymous power which manifests itself in the taboo word 'revolution'. But who marches, invisible, in front of this revolutionary patrol? Here is Blok's reply:

. . . . .

and wrapped in wild snow at their head
carrying a blood-red flag—
soft-footed where the blizzard swirls,

invulnerable where bullets crossed—
crowned with a crown of snowflake pearls,
a flowery diadem of frost,
ahead of them goes Jesus Christ.*

Since my childhood I have loved Alexander Blok. When, because of my beliefs, the Soviet rulers forced me to go into a psychiatric clinic, so as to silence me, I spent many long sleepless nights holding mental dialogues with him. I have thought much about his spiritual tragedy, about the tragedy which made him see in his poetic vision Christ, crowned with thorns, invisibly walk before the Revolution. I would therefore like to quote to the reader that part of my book *Ward Seven,* which could stand as an answer to Blok's *The Twelve*:

Alexander Pushkin (1799 to 1837) is recognized to this day as the greatest Russian poet. His significance lies in the fact that he had no predecessors whose use of the language he could take over and transform for his own use. 'Out of nothing' he created a Russian literary language, using Church-Slavonic and the language of the common people, and creating by this marriage the language which has been used by all great Russian poets to the present day. Pushkin enlarged the classical ideal of art and life through a romantic spiritual attitude. (19th century engraving.)

You were had, I was had,
We were all had—
There were bullets in the night
And success in the morning—
But not for all.
For whom then?

A day is nothing, a day passes,
A day is not for ever—
But man is—he can't take a holiday
from eternity,
Not be, not remember, not feel, not know,
The night steals up like a thief—
Sitting alone in your room, can you hear it?
The mice scrabble,
The jailers jangle their keys—
Quiet, don't scream,
No one will hear us.

Are you thinking about truth and heroes?—
forget all that.
The night comes with confusion,
Illusion, torture and spells—
And where is your Christ
In his crown of red roses?

At dead of night
Twelve executioners
Lead us, the remnant, away to be shot
And at their head
Herod, with a red star on his breast
Confidently leads the elect to the
slaughter.**

* Translations from *Alexander Blok: The Twelve and other Poems,* translated by Jon Stallworthy and Peter France. Eyre Spottiswood, 1970.

** From *Ward 7,* by Valeriy Tarsis, translated by Katya Brown, William Collins Sons.

The hard school of the last decades, and the example of our former failure to act, have at last taught us fundamental lessons. The Russian intelligentsia of today will not come into conflict with a changed Russian State. It will help to realize political and spiritual freedom in Russia, so as to give a proper human meaning to the social and economic advances. Like Dostoevsky, I am convinced that Russia has not yet said her last word in history. I wait and pray for this new, devout Russia of freedom, humanity and peace.

Fyodor Mikhailovitch Dostoevsky (1821 to 1881) is the poet of the Russian God-seekers. Man and his contradictions, his struggle towards freedom, and a personal self-realization form the basic themes of his novels. His existentialist-psychological understanding of his characters has influenced the whole of world literature, and, in the West, was finally developed further in the works of Marcel Proust and James Joyce. As the poet of human destiny seen through Christian thought, he can be compared only to Dante.

Alyosha's Russia

Where is the Russian troika dashing to?—the great Gogol once asked himself this disquieting question. For since the days of Peter the Great, the development of Russia has continued an ever accelerating pace. The runaway horses were absconding with the Tsars and their advisors. Do today's drivers have the troika firmly in hand? And where will it rush to? Pushkin was already moved to write to his companion Peter Tchaadayev the prophetic verses:

Believe, oh friend, one day the sun will rise
Morning-bright with happiness!
Russia will waken from her sleep
And write our names upon the ruined stones
Of despotism overthrown.

With the Bolshevist October Revolution of 1917, the Russian, like Dante before him, began his journey through hell. It is true that the Communists have brought Russia power and world influence which she had previously never had to the same extent. But the price the Russian people have had to pay for this progress has been monstrous. Millions of deported, millions of dead! The retrospective condemnation of the Stalinist dictatorship and Stalinist crimes by people, some of whom had been partly responsible for them or had profited by them in some way, does not eradicate past injustice. Without question the technical advances and successes which Soviet Russia can show do fill the Russian people with pride. Unquestionably the victory over the German invaders in a great patriotic war has been largely thought of as a success brought about by the ability of the regime to co-ordinate Russia's strength. But it is indisputable that despite all outward successes, the Russian people and the Russian individual are not, compared with past times, any happier. The old autocracy of the Tsars has been succeeded by an even more rigorous autocracy of the Party, a party which represents the instrument of power of an oligarchy, a new class which finds its *raison d'être* in the exercise of power.

Lenin understood how to engineer the Russian people's desire for political and social freedom towards support for the Bolshevist Revolution. Fundamentally it is the hope for freedom which has enabled the Russians to tolerate the Bolshevist regime until now. For the Russian people are unendingly patient and long-suffering. However long Russia has to endure under the servitude of the contemporary regime, one thing is certain: the Bolshevist decades are only a stage in the progress towards

Page 205:
This girl does not correspond to the Western conception of the 'typical Russian', yet she is a typical representative of the Russia of today. Her immediate home is Samarkand, the capital of the Uzbek Soviet Republic. The Uzbeks are descended from the Turks, a living contrast with the original Russians who founded the Russian State and made it into a great social structure embracing many nations.

Pages 206/207:
The well-known Soviet sculptor Maniser is the prototype of the conforming artist. Most of his works are portraits of Soviet politicians. His adaptability contrasts with those spiritually and artistically creative people who affirm their responsibility to themselves and prove their unconforming fearlessness.

Pages 208/209:
These two men represent the span of Russian humanity. Left: the chemist and Nobel Prize winner Semyonov, a sensitive scholar. Right: a Shevsurian peasant in national costume. He radiates the native strength and calm of the eternal peasant, and guarantees the spiritual and physical vitality of the Russian State.

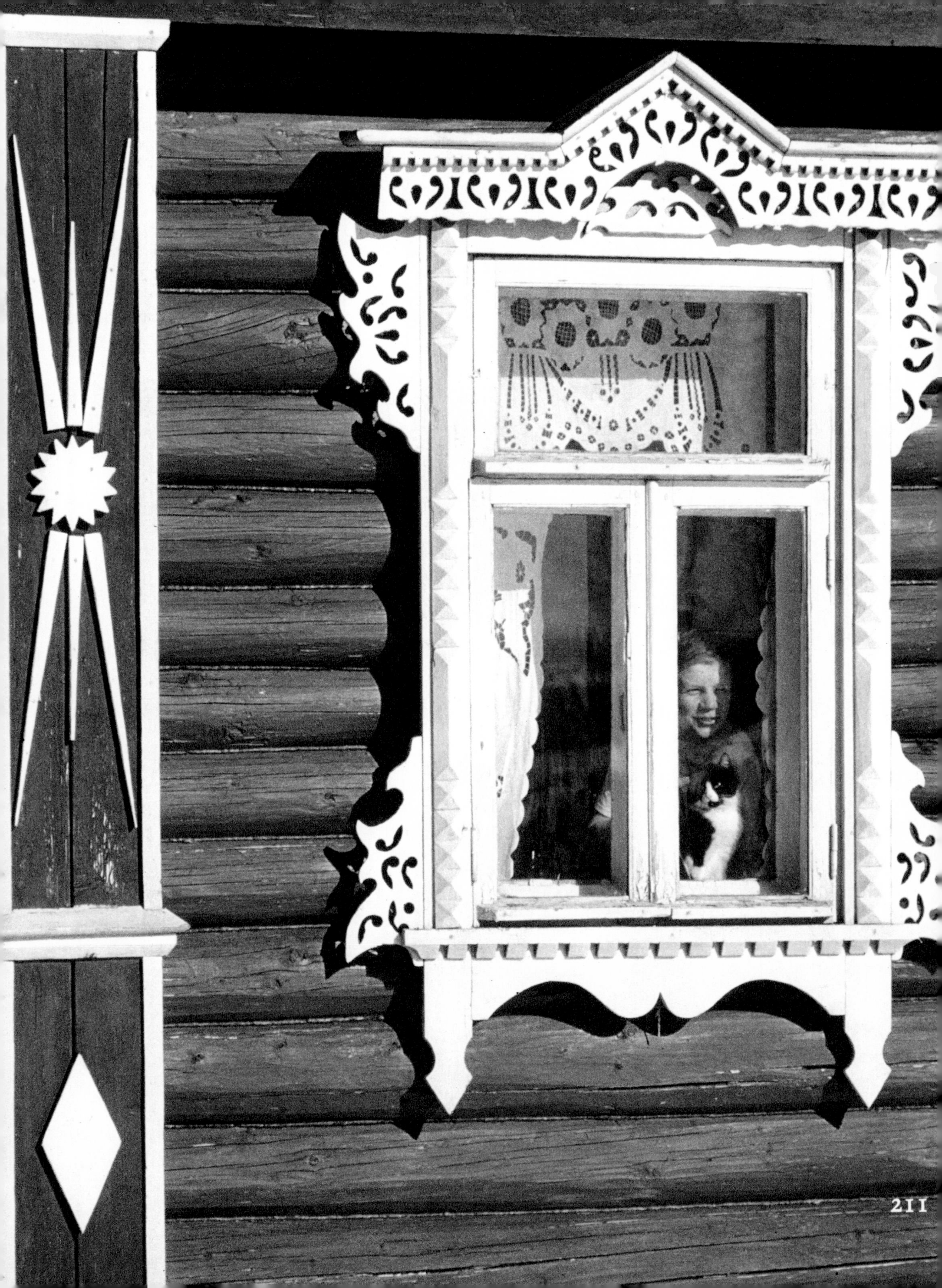

freedom. The Russian does not want the formal freedom which seems so desirable to the West European. He longs for a life which is free in itself, for a life enhancing human dignity, not measured by material or social standards.

I have already alluded to the fact that the three legitimate sons of old Karamazov embody the three facets of the Russian character. In the Bolshevist era, Ivan, who through his passionate seeking of God became an atheist, and his illegitimate half-brother, Smerdyakov, who oozes with loathsome servility, came into their own. In the spiritual wrestling between Ivan and Alyosha, it is the pious and devout Alyosha who takes the burdens and sorrows of his brothers upon himself, who dreams of the marriage of Cana beside the coffin of the Elder Zossima, and perceives the secret which is hidden in the changing of water into wine. Alyosha wakes from his dream, leaves the coffin and steps into the open air. 'His soul, overflowing with rapture, was craving for freedom and unlimited space. The vault of heaven, studded with softly shining stars, stretched wide and vast over him.... The silence of the earth seemed to merge into the silence of the heavens, the mystery of the earth came into contact with the mystery of the stars.... It was as though the threads from all those innumerable worlds of God met all at once in his soul, and it was trembling all over "as it came in contact with other worlds". He wanted to forgive everyone and everything.... He had fallen upon the earth a weak youth, but he rose from it a resolute fighter for the rest of his life....'

Alyosha's Russia is coming—full of burning impatience and unshakeable hope. I await the day of this epiphany.

Pages 210/211:
The front of a multi-storey building in Moscow's Lenin Avenue contrasts with the small idyllic house in a Russian village. The patterned curtains, the sawn-wood window facings make a great contrast with the architecture of prefabricated buildings of our day.

Pages 212/213:
To 'celebrate a feast day whenever one occurs' is an old Slavonic proverb. In the picture on the left the Muscovites are celebrating a festival in the parks of Moscow, gay and untroubled. This 'worldly' gaiety is contrasted with a midnight mass at Easter in a Moscow church.

Pages 214/215:
Most married women in the Soviet Union have jobs. Many factories have crèches and play-grounds where the children remain until the parents finish work.

Page 216:
Young girl, representative of Russian youth. The Soviet youth of today seem more sober, free of prejudice and more objective than in the past. They do not question the Communist State as such, but they are critical of many of the characteristics of the Soviet regime.

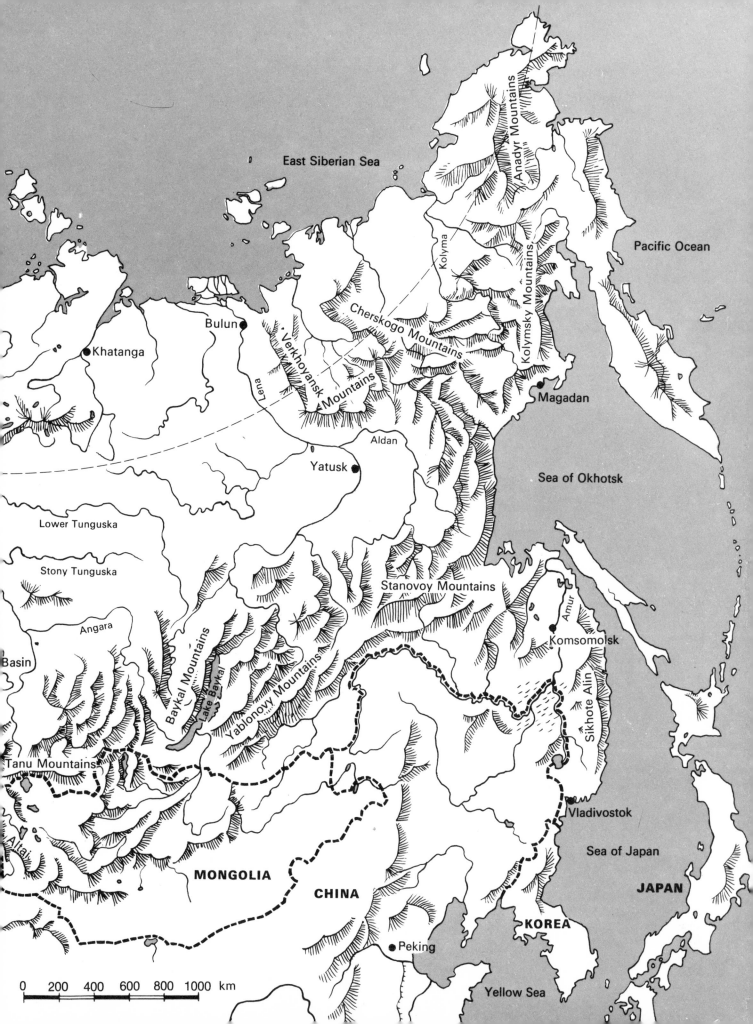

East Siberian Sea

Pacific Ocean

Anadyr Mountains

Kolyma

Kolymsky Mountains

Cherskogo Mountains

Bulun

Khatanga

Verkhoyansk Mountains

Lena

Magadan

Aldan

Yatusk

Sea of Okhotsk

Lower Tunguska

Stony Tunguska

Stanovoy Mountains

Angara

Amur

Komsomolsk

Basin

Baykal Mountains

Lake Baykal

Yablonovy Mountains

Sikhote Alin

Tanu Mountains

Altai

Vladivostok

Sea of Japan

MONGOLIA

CHINA

JAPAN

KOREA

Peking

Yellow Sea

0   200   400   600   800   1000   km

ILLUSTRATION ACKNOWLEDGMENTS

APN-Photo: 198
Archiv: 17, 82, 160, 190/191
Mario de Biasi/Mondadori Press: 159, 161
Camera Press: 24, 60/61, 78, 84, 98/99, 106,
    126/127, 140/141, 144/145
Cornel Capa: 20, 197
L. Dukas: 72/73, 103, 109, 110/111, 112,
    112/113, 116, 128/129, 132, 158, 167
Douglas Glass/Dukas: 14
Burt Glinn/Magnum: 40, 43, 46, 46/47, 48/49,
    54, 59, 62, 74, 93, 104, 105, 125, 136, 155,
    199, 200, 206/207, 208, 209, 210, 211, 212,
    213, 214, 215, 216
Swen-Eric Hedin: 18/19, 44, 130/131, 142/143,
    148
Stig T. Karlsson/Tio: 70/71
Keystone: 11
William Klein: 39, 52
Len Sirman: 36/37, 51, 68, 68/69, 80/81, 83,
    94/95, 114/115, 133, 134, 135, 142, 143, 149,
    156/157, 168/169, 170, 182/183, 205

Fred Meier: 181, 188/189
Angela Neuke: 45, 47, 79, 186/187
Georg Oddner/Tio: 33
Lennard Olson/Tio: 67
Picturepoint Ltd.: 12/13, 139, 150
Seeliger/Stern: 20/21, 21, 34, 35, 38, 50, 53,
    100, 146, 146/147, 147, 184/185
Howard Sochurek: 96/97
John Massey Stewart/Picturepoint: 22/23, 162
Studio Vista Ltd.: 77
Alfred Waldis: 192

Text illustrations:
Archiv: 6, 26, 122, 172, 176, 179
Staatsbibliothek Berlin, Bildarchiv (Handke):
    30, 31, 56, 64, 86, 90, 118, 120, 174, 178, 195,
    202, 203
Studio Vista Ltd.: 8, 64
Wiemann: 9